Blackbird

Blackbird

Betty Winston Baye

Betty Baye
3/07

August Press
Newport News, Va.

BLACKBIRD

For information, address August Press,
P.O. Box 6693,
Newport News, VA 23606.
www.augustpress.net

Cover photo by Keith Williams
Cover design by Rob King

ISBN   0-9635720-3-2

Library of Congress   96-083944

First edition

10 9 8 7 6 5 4 3 2 1

To my family

Mommy and Daddy: I'll live forever in your wisdom and your love. It aches as if you just left yesterday.

Debbie and Georgeann: It's the three of us forever, through thick and through thin, just like Mommy always said.

Darnell, Larry, Bernadette, Tinisha Janell and Dayvon: Take it from Aunt Betty, there's nothing more important than that you be good men and good women.

Bernard: Thanks for giving me nieces and rides whenever I needed them.

Roosevelt [1952-2000]: Thanks for loving Debbie and for bringing me bagels, cream cheese and coffee.

Contents

Preface

Jackie Early wrote a poem 30 years ago when we were members of the National Black Theater in Harlem. My friend's words still inspire me.
The poem's most memorable lines were:

You call me black.
I know. I know.
I call myself black, now, too!

Those words were an affirmation, a mantra.
They were another way of saying, "Black is beautiful" when it badly needed to be said. So many people, unfortunately even many black people, are programmed not to think so.
It's important for all parents to instill high self-esteem in their children. But it's essential for children of color. Otherwise, they won't survive and thrive in a cruel and color-conscious world.
So many children fail, not because they lack the smarts, but because they're not conditioned to believe in themselves. Instead, they are conditioned to believe that they're ugly and worthless and to act accordingly.
Like everyone, I have moments of self-doubt, but I rebound when I go inside myself and remember who and whose I am. I get up, dust myself off and get back in to the race when I remember that I was blessed to have been nurtured by elders, who loved, kissed and cuddled me and who affirmed me, saying, in effect: "You're somebody, Betty. You are beautiful, and most important of all, you are God's child, and God don't make junk."
I've titled this, my second book, Blackbird, to honor my village.
The redbird, bluebird and yellowbird are all beautiful, but I'm a blackbird, who was raised in an eagle's nest.
Before college, career and awards, I was fitted with wings and taught how to fly by incredibly loving, creative and courageous black people, whose opportunities for greatness outside our black world were limited by color and circumstance.

I can do nothing more important with my life than to make my village proud.

I want my ancestors and elders to be assured that I really did absorb their lessons and their pain in even feeling it necessary to teach them. Maybe something I do, something I say or something that I write will be a balm for

their wounds. Maybe the words will help right some of the wrongs done to my elders by people for whom they were just "the help," insignificant and invisible.

I can imagine no other reason for God to have allowed me to become a writer, for the late James Aronoson of Hunter College to put me on this path, than

to bring the news from my village to a larger world.

What you have in your hand consists primarily of selected columns that were first published in The Courier-Journal in Louisville and subsequently in newspapers nationwide. I don't imagine that every single column in this book

will resonate with every single reader; that's too much to expect. But I hope that every single reader manages to find at least one sentiment in this book with which they can identify and wish to share with others.

Finally, I'm blessed that my book has found its way into your hands. If you purchase it for yourself or a loved one, it'll be for me, like Jackie's poem, an affirmation that will inspire me to write on.

Betty

August 2000
Louisville, Ky.

A libation to my elders and friends

LAST YEAR I was a Nieman Fellow at Harvard University. Often, as I trekked across Harvard Yard on my way to class, I couldn't help but think about how long a trip it had been from East Harlem, NY to Cambridge, MA.

History clings to Harvard. It's what gives the school its ambiance and its students their sense of place and purpose.

During quiet moments, I'd sit in my small apartment on Harvard Street, by the sea at Cape Cod, at a friend's home on Martha's Vineyard, or in a restaurant in Newport, RI, and contemplate my history. I'd remember the saying that in order to know where you're going, you've got to know where you've been.

This is about my history. It's a libation to my elders and friends and speaks to my implicit understanding that I am not self-created. Rather, I've been showered with good fortune. I've walked gracefully in high heels through doors kicked open by barefoot people with little or no education.

In my quiet New England moments, I'd remember how my parents, George and Betty Winston, made a way out of no way. I'd remember the Christmas of 1955 when my family was burned out and left homeless and how Miss Anna Mae and her husband, Carey, who had so many children crammed in so little space, invited us to come stay with them. I'd remember the days when dinner was boiled rice and chicken feet and when entertainment was my parents playing bid whist under a street lamp.

page 1

I'd remember Father Kilmer Meyers, the Episcopal priest who worked the system and got my family an apartment in the projects and money to buy second-hand furniture.

In my quiet up north, I'd think about the boys and girls I grew up with, and I'd wonder why God had sent me out into the world, like a scout, to experience what was going on and then go back and tell the people left behind.

In my New England solitude, I'd celebrate my parents, for whom neither poverty nor blackness nor femaleness was an excuse for not always doing my best. I'd think about how my father loved me so and bragged to anyone who'd listen that his daughter was a college graduate and a writer. I'd remember the time when Daddy walked miles to work because he'd given me his last 15 cents to buy a steno book.

And of course, there's Mommy. She is simply the smartest woman I know. She's my best friend and rarely ends our long-distance conversations without saying, "I love you!" I can't imagine the day when I won't be able to call Mommy and hear her say, "It's going to be OK, baby. You'll see."

When I grow up I'd like to be like my mother. I envy her quick wit, her incredible common sense, her commitment to family, and her wonderfully salty tongue that can respond to a deliberate insult with quick and decisive speed.

What can I say about Sarah Pinder Newkirk, my godmother? When I was young and very poor, she always made sure that I had pretty dresses to wear to school and took the pressure off my parents by taking me with her to Philadelphia and Tampa in the summers.

Oh, how I loved my late Uncle Artie and Aunt Catherine, who long before James Brown sang, "I'm black and I'm proud," called me a black beauty.

And everyone should have an Aunt Evelyn and Uncle Charles Rheubottom. Long before I could afford vacations in Europe, the Caribbean or Mexico, my uncle and aunt allowed me to rest at their place, known within our family as "Rheubottom Estates" in teeny, tiny Sykesville, Md.

Often, when I sat still in New England, I'd wonder what I

would have become had I not been befriended by Ralph Featherstone, Mae Jackson, James Lytle, Irving Davis, James Forman, Elombe Brath, Lyn Dozier, Duane Jones, Francis Hyman, James Aronson and Arnold Gibbons, and others inside and outside the civil rights movement. They taught me how to struggle. But more important, they taught me how to get back on my feet after some fool had tap-danced on my dreams.

I'm a collection of all these folks.

And as I write this, my first column, I think of you, the reader. I'm humbled and excited to have your ear. I hope you'll enjoy what I have to say and that I never become so full of myself that I take you for granted or insult your intelligence. Of course, I'd love it if you and I would always agree. But that's not sensible since we all view life through different glasses. My hope is that you and I will be able to agree to disagree agreeably.

– Sept. 19, 1991

Prayer is in the heart

MY CUP runneth over.

That line of the 23rd Psalm soothes me now-much as I was comforted when Mommy would treat my colds by massaging me with Vicks Vapo Rub.

In 20 years as a journalist, I've written hundreds of thousands of words.

Still, I cannot tell it all. I cannot adequately convey all that God has done and continues to do for me.

But the words "my cup runneth over" comes pretty close.

Last Sunday morning, the Rev. Clay Calloway, an assistant pastor at my church, St. Stephen Baptist Church, sounded a similar theme. He didn't preach long, but he preached strong about prayer, about the countless ways one can pray:

Kneeling. Standing. Running. Walking. Reclining. While combing your hair.

page 4

While getting dressed. In the car. On the job.

If you cut out my tongue, I can grunt a prayer, Calloway said. Amen, brother.

I'm sure that's why it doesn't alarm me when some complain that prayer has been taken out of the schools. Truly prayerful people don't need permission; they just pray.

Prayer shouldn't be about display, but conviction. I've been taught that God hears a simple, quiet, private prayer no less than He does one that is thundered from the rooftop.

I wonder, too, how many of those who object to the absence of public prayer in the schools actually pray daily with their children before hustling the kids into the car or onto the school bus.

Even without the rest of the 23rd Psalm wrapped around them, "my cup runneth over" constitutes a prayer.

Of course, I didn't fully comprehend this soothing, affirming statement until life had taught me a thing or two. I had to be humbled and broken, and I had to face up to the many contradictions that can reside inside one soul.

I've always been especially impressed by those who proclaim my cup runneth over when, materially at least, they have little. Still, they pray.

My cup runneth over sounds so poignant in this season of excess; this season where exaggerated joy about baubles, priceless or not, cannot fill the void in an empty heart.

I was deep in my Christmas state of mind when a letter arrived that momentarily pricked my good spirits. The missive contained an addendum: "Of course, not for publication."

Writing from an Anchorage, Ky., address, the correspondent begged to differ with a column in which I pointed out some of the terrible injustices in the criminal justice system, including the stream of death row indigents who have been released once decent attorneys proved that they were innocent. But the writer felt obliged to let me know that, while hearts like mine bleed, he or she celebrated an execution in Texas.

Bravo that Robert Atworth was rather speedily put to death, the writer gloated. A confessed murderer, Atworth committed his cold and dirty deed in 1995.

Usually, there are more than four years from arrest to execution, and what a savings to taxpayers that in this case, at least, "there apparently were no drawn out appeals," the writer said.

But I'm not ashamed to be a bleeding heart, because I know that somebody bled and died for me. Can my heart bleed any less than the heart that bled for me; the heart that beat like that of any other human, and whose life and ministry, often among the left-outs, scoundrels and murderers of His time, is the real reason for the season?

Centuries ago, just like now, some delighted in executions. I first heard as a child the story of those who screamed "Crucify! Crucify!" and who, when even Pontius Pilate was a little reluctant, insisted, "Away with him. Away with him. Crucify him."

Atworth may not be the child who was born in a manger, but Atworth assuredly, as even murderers are, was a child of God.

What is striking is how the spirit of spite and unforgiveness can rest so comfortably inside so many, whose cups runneth over and whose own sins, perhaps not murder but sins nonetheless, have been forgiven time and time again.

Were I to wake up Christmas morning with nary a gift under my tree, it would still be a glorious day-another for me to stretch my hands to the heavens, weep for my dearly beloved departed and say to the four walls, "My cup runneth over."

— December 23, 1999

A distorted view from the pew

THE REV. Henry Lyons, leader of the 8.5 million-member National Baptist Convention USA, has badly lost his way. In July, his wife of 25 years, reputedly in jealous rage, which she now denies, set fire to the $700,000 home she discovered was jointly owned by her husband and another woman. At the time Deborah Lyons was being arrested in Florida, the "other woman," convicted embezzler Bernice Jones Edwards, was in Africa with Henry Lyons.

Later, it was discovered that Henry Lyons and Edwards had other joint holdings, including a $135,000 Mercedes-Benz and a time-share property at Lake Tahoe, and that the two may have financed these goodies, at least in part, with money intended for the National Baptist Convention.

Then came reports that Lyons was abusive, had fathered two children out of wedlock, and claimed he "forgot" about his two marriages prior to marrying Deborah Lyons in 1972. Lyons also may be in hot water for lobbying members of Congress on behalf of Nigerian strong man Sonny Abacha but failing to register as a foreign agent.

Lyons, needless to say, has a lot of explaining to do. And that "exclusive" he recently gave to the black media is worse than "lame."

The Bible does say that anyone who is without sin should cast the first stone, and, frankly, my hands are full. But Henry Lyons hardly strikes a sympathetic pose, especially when he sinks to blaming white folks for his troubles.

If anything, Lyons' predicament may be a manifestation of something insidious: Some churches have gone from being God-centered to preacher-centered. That happens when the preacher can do no wrong, and trustees and others are reduced to babbling idiots programmed to say yes to anything the preacher asks for.

How is it possible for someone as highly placed as Henry Lyons, pastor of Bethel Metropolitan Church in St. Petersburg, Fla., to be so reckless and for so many to now profess ignorance?

Preacher worship? Or some Baptist rendition of the military's "Don't ask, don't tell" rule?

If Henry Lyons is so tragically flawed, when did it all begin? Assuredly, it was not the moment Deborah Lyons struck a match or flicked a Bic.

No one is perfect, but don't all preachers know that being a role model is part of the deal? How in heaven's name did Henry Lyons get so mired in this mess? Preacher worship?

What part of her soul did Deborah Lyons exchange for the honorary position of silently suffering "first lady"?

And is Bernice Edwards really Eve, Jezebel and Delilah-the devil in a red dress who conned Henry Lyons into doing what he ought not to have done?

I can't understand why the women of the church were silent. When I talked to my pastor, the Rev. Kevin W. Cosby, about my concerns, he said some preachers often use the Bible "to perpetuate patriarchy and to maintain male control."

Black church women, Cosby said, tend to "have a high regard for the Bible, and traditionally they aren't going to do anything they believe is against the will of God." And God's will "is being interpreted for women from the perspective of males. . . ."

However, Cosby said, "to make patriarchal interpretations synonymous with God's Word is idolatry."

I doubt that I'll ever meet the definition of ideal held by some church women. You see my faith informs me that we ought to be challenging Pharoah anywhere, anytime-in our homes, on our jobs, in our communities and in our pulpits.

Had more men and women of faith stood against preacher worship in the church, Henry Lyons might not be in his predicament.

– September 4, 1997

A man who listens to women

I DON'T recall which crisis of the spirit prompted a friend to stop by my place one night just to talk.

But whatever the reason, at some point she, a preacher's daughter, fished out of her purse several folded, photocopied pages from T. D. Jakes' book Woman, *Thou Art Loosed.* She handed them over as if they were a beautifully wrapped gift that she couldn't wait for me to open. And it was a gift.

Jakes, pastor of Potter's House in Dallas, is a rarity in the male preaching fraternity. He actually listens to women.

And so it struck me as a shortcoming that *The Wall Street Journal's* profile of Jakes didn't answer the essential question: What makes a woman who'll walk 10 miles for a 50-percent-off sale hand over $20 for videotapes of Jakes' sermons and for his books?

It's insufficient, I believe, to say simply that Jakes is charming, grandiose and is "both thrilling and persuasive" with his empowerment message for broken people. Such attributes are not novelties in black churches.

I am aware that *The Wall Street Journal* prides itself as a newspaper primarily for the business crowd. And when I saw the headline "Prophet Motives" on the Jakes article, I knew what to expect, and even imagined how the article probably came about.

Someone wondered whether Jakes, an African American, is a charlatan.

Last year, his church took in more than $20 million, and Jakes personally, according to *The Journal,* earns millions from book and record deals, the details of which he won't disclose.

Still, despite their business bent, *The Wall Street Journal* editors should also have filled readers in with more specifics about Jakes' rise to matinee idol status.

After all, Jakes is not a looker like Denzel Washington or Leonardo DiCaprio. And to be sure, lots of preachers have charisma.

T. D. Jakes is getting rich largely because he knows that men, preachers foremost among them, have a nasty habit of not listening to women-not their wives, not their co-workers, not their congregants. Many men also don't pay attention to what women are saying when they're not talking.

Jakes taps into women who are skilled at hiding themselves in church, work, the family and volunteerism. He pays attention to their loneliness, neediness and distress, which may be hidden behind gossamer veils of duty and "good works."

He shows compassion when he stands women up in front of their mirrors and says look at what you've become. And then he encourages women and offers tips on how they can survive and thrive. This is necessary because, even in our culture, women are deemed "lesser" than men.

Jakes knows the women who stay on their knees because they are unable to stand up. In his book *The Lady, Her Lover, and Her Lord*, Jakes speaks to women who are bent, not from without, but from within. He speaks to their "deep, dark secrets and traumas that have left them twisted and misfigured.

Issues, relationships and incidents leap out of their past and hold them hostage, forever chained to emotional pain..." They are women whose "wounds might not be fresh" but who still hurt because they have never really healed.

So it's not simply marketing savvy; T. D. Jakes has listened very well.

What's more, he appears to have learned some important things from his mother, his wife and the other women around him.

His big attraction is his much appreciated willingness to pay close attention to the issues that women the world over confront all the time. But now he has been discovered.

The question, of course, is whether a country preacher can be a fabulously successful entrepreneur and not be corrupted.

We've seen many who have not passed the test. Most recently and notoriously, there was the Rev. Henry Lyons, president of the National Baptist Convention U.S.A., who has been jailed for misappropriating hundreds of thousands of dollars from his convention and his church.

For some, the verdict on Jakes is already in. "He's basically telling people what they want to hear; it's a con job," said one preacher cited by The Journal.

That may be, but the Trinity Foundation, a televangelist watchdog group, told *The Wall Street Journal* that there's no "hint" that Jakes' worldly gains are ill-gotten.

People are probably right to say that T. D. Jakes is full of himself. But we all know that what's considered arrogant by some people is deemed brilliance by others.

T. D. Jakes takes the notion of the sensitive man to a higher level, and women love him for it. His message to men is simple: Pay attention and you, too, may be richly rewarded. You may not become wealthy, but you'll gain love, admiration and respect from the women in your lives.

– September 10, 1998

A comforting lesson from an on-time God

Christmas is the time when Christians focus on a miraculous birth that occurred more than 2,000 years ago when our Savior, Jesus of Nazareth, was born.

Christmas is the season when, in sermon and song, Christians reflect on our values, and none more so than that God so loved humanity that He "sent his only begotten Son into the world that we might live through him."

So it was appropriate that on pre-Christmas Sunday, the theme of Sunday school at my church was "Celebrating God's Love." I didn't realize until after church just how relevant and comforting this particular message would be in my life.

As soon as I arrived home from church, my phone rang. It was my sister Debbie, calling to inform me that Uncle Lonnie had died. The words were no sooner out of Debbie's mouth than I was reminded that whenever I resist the temptation to simply worship at "Bedside Baptist," I end up being particularly blessed by a Sunday school lesson, a song, a sermon or an encouraging word.

Maybe others have felt what I often have, which is that on certain Sundays, my pastor

page 12

seems to peer down into my soul to discover the precise words I need to hear to help get me through the hour, the day and the week.

So it was on Sunday morning, when I was in church and filled with the spirit of the season – and when my uncle was laid out on his cooling board in a Richmond, VA, hospital.

Every death and birth is significant. In most families, either event changes the molecules, so to speak.

And when an elder dies, all who are under him, or in the next generation, move up a step closer still to our own dates with destiny.

Uncle Lonnie's death is the end of the Winstons of his generation. He was the last of my father's sisters and brothers-the last of George and Minnie Belle Winston's children. He arrived at that status in 1994, when Uncle Gerald, the youngest of the clan, died of complications related to Parkinson's Disease.

And because he was the last, the nieces and nephews tended to make a special fuss over Uncle Lonnie, and he loved it.

It never occurred to me that maybe Uncle Lonnie might be a wee bit lonely, having to go on without his mother, father, or sisters and brothers.

Even children, as special as children tend to be, cannot stand in the stead of siblings. They're bound by events and by secrets that are stashed within their generation, which they talk about only when others aren't around.

When I spoke with Uncle Lonnie a few weeks ago, I told him of my intention to buy a videocamera for Christmas and said that it and I were coming to Richmond after the holidays so that I could record him talking about the Winston family.

My intention was to add Uncle Lonnie's recollections to the information my cousin, Caroline Winston, has been collecting from various sources in Richmond, including courthouse records, old newspaper clippings, and church bulletins. I knew that Uncle Lonnie was a rich resource because, other than during his military service, he had stayed home in Virginia.

Our interview, of course, will not come to pass. And isn't that how it often happens when a loved one dies? We survivors reflect on the many missed opportunities we had to embrace and to say, "I love you."

But still, I have no regrets.

My relationship with Uncle Lonnie was warm. Forever etched in my memory is the first time I laid eyes on him. I couldn't have been more than 5 or 6 when Uncle Lonnie visited us in New York.

He cut a dashing pose in his Air Force uniform, and when he looked down at me and smiled, it was love at first sight. Uncle Lonnie was the most handsome man other than my father that I had ever seen. He was average height, though he seemed a giant at the time, and was smooth and dark like those ice cream treats that are covered by a thin layer of sweet chocolate. And Uncle Lonnie's voice had a certain texture and pitch that always made me feel warm inside.

His sweet voice has been silenced.

But my faith sustains me. It is faith that has carried me through all the losses in recent years that have removed from me many of the pillars of my life, many of the bridges that have carried me safely across: my father, my mother, my godmother, other uncles, aunts and elder friends.

So it was prophetic, I'd like to believe, that on Sunday morning when my Uncle Lonnie was dying, that I was in church, where I was supposed to be; where I need to be.

My faith informs me that physical death is not the end. John 3:16 counsels Christians that God gave His only son and that whosoever believes in Him shall not perish, but shall have eternal life.

I've got to believe that a day will come when I will see Uncle Lonnie and all the others again. Above all others, that thought will make this Christmas merry, in spite of this temporary grief.

--December 25, 1997

Chapter Two:

Kinfolks

A gift from a grateful daughter

Dear Mommy:

It is your day again. And as you know, lots of money will be spent on flowers, dinners and Mother's Day cards. I've done those things before. But being you, Mommy, you complain about the money I "waste" on such things when, as you say, the best Mother's Day gift is just knowing that your children are happy and healthy.

So this year, Mommy, rather than leaving it up to the professional card writers, I thought I'd speak for myself. Decided to say what I want to say in my own words, believing that you'll appreciate them, as no doubt many mothers might, much more than the words of Hallmark.

First, Mommy, thanks for the lessons-the lessons I've learned as I've watched you parent Debbie, Georgeann and me. What a challenge it must be to try to be a parent to three grown, strong-willed women, who every now and again get the notion that we're smarter than you just because we're younger, we've traveled more and we know more people.

Yet I'm still impressed, Mommy, at how, even when we are full of ourselves, you dispense advice, making it clear that since we're all grown, we can take that advice or leave it. I imagine there are plenty of moments, Mommy, when it seems to you that we're not listening.

But as the oldest of your three girls it's fair to say that you do get through. You've always gotten through. It's just that sometimes our egos don't allow us to just admit, "Mommy, you were right." Sometimes our egos don't allow us to easily come clean and say, "Mommy, what you said would happen did."

I know you've gotten through. I can't tell you how many hundreds of nights I've lain in my bed weeping and saying, "Mommy sure was right!"

I also know you've gotten through because I look at myself and Debbie and Georgeann. Now, we're a long way from perfect, but we're decent women. We try hard not to forget what we learned as children: Don't lie; don't cheat, don't steal, and don't ever be jealous of what others have because we don't know what they had to do to get it or what they have to do to keep it. We are no doubt the women we are because of the woman you are.

And another thing, Mommy. I bet you didn't know that when I was young I really believed that everybody's mother was like mine. You always said that I can be naive about many things.

But Mommy, for the longest time I believed that all mothers and daughters had the relationship, the friendship, the love that you and I share.

I believed that everyone's mother cared about how they looked when they went off to school, paid attention to the time they arrived home, and helped them with their multiplication tables.

Remember, Mommy, how you'd sit at the kitchen table for hours at a time, saying, "How much is nine times nine? How much is eight times five?" I know you got frustrated, but you never yelled when I didn't get the right answer since you knew that I was trying my very best. That was always good enough.

But life has taught me, Mommy, that millions of kids don't have mothers like you. And you were a teenage mom, just 19 when I was born.

The point, Mommy, is that I see so many people, way too many, just stumbling through life and falling into holes they can't get out of because they've missed out on the basics. They're stumbling along because they've missed out on the little things many of us take for granted, like a mother who for no special reason just says, "Baby, you're mine and I love you."

I guess, Mommy, that's why this old world feels so mean to me and as if it's getting meaner every day. Everywhere I look, Mommy, I see people who've never been touched, never been taught right from wrong, never learned, as I have, the truth of the statement, "If you don't stand up for something, you'll fall for anything."

I look around, Mommy, and I'm eternally grateful that God gave me a mother and father to teach me to be compassionate for others who have less, no matter how little I have.

In these, my middle years, I know that it's the basics, those lessons learned early on, that allow us to manage and get through life's challenges and dilemmas. Whoever first said that we learn every important thing that we really need to know by a fairly young age was absolutely correct. All the things I've learned since, Mommy, are simply the frosting on a cake that was already baked.

Meanwhile, Mommy, have I told you lately that I think you're absolutely, positively, the wisest woman I know. And guess what? The older I get, the wiser you seem to be. I suppose I'll never quite catch up to your knowledge, Mommy, because whatever I learn, you've learned it already.

So, Betty Jane Brown Winston, have a great day! And remember: No matter where I am or where you are, know that I'll be loving you.

– May 7, 1992

Peeking inside Mommy's closet

FOR YEARS, Mommy resisted pleas to explore a particular closet in her apartment.

So when she finally relented, my sister Georgeann and I got busy. And what didn't we find in Mommy's closet! The effort made me realize anew why God put mothers on earth: to love and protect us, of course, and to whisper "well done" when others insist that we're poor excuses for human beings.

It's mother wit, not academic achievement, that enables mothers to easily spot sadness and vulnerability behind our big smiles and boastful talk.

God also put mothers here to save stuff that, in our immaturity, has little or no value.

Mommy's closet was a treasure trove. It yielded old photographs, report cards, diplomas, merit certificates, and the citation for bravery Georgeann earned for pulling a disabled neighbor to safety from a burning apartment.

Out of Mommy's closet tumbled caps and tassles from our various graduations.

Mommy had even saved copies of the Benjamin Franklin High School newspapers related to my campaign to be senior class secretary. My winning campaign slogan, a play on the family name, was: "Don't vote Camel or Chesterfield, just vote Winston and get a good deal!"

Old funeral programs stored in the closet should squelch sometimes heated arguments about who was born when and died when, where, and of what.

A real gem we uncovered was a March 7, 1955, letter to my parents from the New York City Housing Authority. They were instructed to bring "at least $77.50," their last rent, gas and electric receipts, and a written income verification to complete our family's application to move into public housing. Despite generally negative perceptions of public housing today, when my family moved into East River Houses in 1955, it was a big step up from the cold-water flats we had drifted in and out of.

To us, East River Houses was paradise. The apartments had smooth brick walls, steam heat and private baths. The amenities included intercoms, playgrounds, elevators and hallways that were kept sparkling clean.

And we knew that our apartment was special because often, in violation of our lease, down-on-their-luck relatives and friends passed through. Back then, the only homeless people we were aware of were Bowery bums. Families and close friends sharing space was common. The motto was "Family in need is family, indeed!"

Considering how often I've changed addresses during the last 30 years, it's amazing that my mother and father-until his death in 1983 – occupied the same four and one-half rooms for 40 years.

The initial rent for Apt. 2A was $52.25 a month. "That was a fortune back then," Mommy said when I showed her the old letter Georgeann and I had taken from her closet.

Also in the closet were some of my father's pay stubs. My sister and I marveled at how our parents had managed, in New York City in the 1960s, to raise a family of five on my father's take-home pay of less than $100 a week. In fact, my family was one of the more fortunate in East River Houses.

Many of my friends' families had even less money coming in and more mouths to feed. The Whites, for example, had 22 kids. The Wilkinsons, who lived across the courtyard, had about 15 children. The McCulloughs, with a musician-father, were struggling to make it with seven kids.

My biggest kick rummaging through Mommy's closet was seeing the absolute joy on her face as I read two 40-year-old letters to her from my grandmother.

Grandma kept Mommy up on family doings because she knew we rarely could afford the bus fare from New York to Maryland.

In one letter, Grandma asked Mommy to pray for her because she was being treated for a heart condition. "You never know," Grandma wrote ominously.

Obviously, the prayers were answered because Grandma lived into her 90s.

The journey into Mommy's closet made this Mother's Day my happiest ever. It was a testimony to how difficult it is to know where you are going in life without an understanding of where you and your people have been.

The treasures in Mommy's closet helped me appreciate anew that success cannot be defined by outsiders, but by people who know how far you've journeyed.

And that's what made the journey into Mommy's closet, and into our family's past, so awfully special. We reconnected with each other, to hard times, to sad times, and times when life couldn't have been better.

At their essence, the treasures my sister and I excavated from our mother's closet reminded us that we're descendants of good people, decent people, hard-working people who carved a way out of no way-and expect us to do the same.

– May 18, 1995

Giving thanks for the eagles

IF I COULD, on this Thanksgiving Day I would convene a gathering of eagles.

It's important to do that every once in a while-to call up for celebration all the people in our lives who have contributed to our wings.

I'd call up my grandparents. What I wouldn't give to celebrate Thanksgiving one more time in their house in Union Bridge, Md. Oh, to bite into one of my grandmother Roxie Key Brown's homemade rolls or to pat her sweet face. How utterly delightful it would be to scoot up on Grandpa's lap and laugh like a fiend as he tickles me.

To hear Aunt Catherine sing a few bars of "Evening Shadows Make Me Blue."

To witness pure joy flood Aunt Evelyn's face as my cousin Freddy serenades her on his organ.

What I wouldn't give on this day to see my father's smile again, to catch his wink and hear him call out, "Boopie Girl." Or to dial Philadelphia and hear my godmother say: "Hi Baby. Howya doing? Me? I'm just fine." Sarah was always fine, even when she really wasn't. If I only had the power, today I would convene a gathering of the eagles.

page 21

I'd love to be able to tell Uncle Gerald, Uncle Artie, Uncle Butt, Uncle Alfred and Uncle Freddy about all the places I've been and the people I've met since they've been gone. I bet their eyes would widen, and one of them would say: "Well, I'll be; I'll just be."

I long for my folks, not uncommon among those whose careers keep them far from home. Whenever I get sentimental, I call the elders of my family.

Sometimes I call my mother twice a day. We talked last week about "the good old days" when she and I were growing up together.

"Do you miss those days, Mama?"

"Oh, God, yes," she said, her voice breaking across the miles. "What a fine time we had, Mama, Papa and all of us."

"All of us" used to include my mother's nine siblings, assorted in-laws, my father, and a passel of nieces, nephews and cousins.

Uncle Tom, in Westminster, Md., is the last of the brothers-in-law. He recalled a Thanksgiving long ago when my grandfather "misplaced" the bottle of Four Roses he had hidden from my grandmother behind the kitchen stove.

"Pop asked, 'Roxie, where is my whisky?' And she said, 'Well, Papa, I don't drink, so why are you asking me?' Then Pop said, 'Well, I guess it evaporated then?' And your grandmother said, 'Well, I guess it did.' "

Uncle Tom laughed hard. And in my mind's eye, I witnessed the confrontation: Petite Grandma saying her piece gently but conveying her dismay that Grandpa nipped at all. And Grandpa, embarrassed at being found out, roaring, but not too loudly, to remind everyone that he was still a lion and the king of his domain.

Listening to Uncle Tom, I remembered how it was when everything and everybody seemed to have a place and how few people actually disturbed the peace.

For example, Uncle Tom told me about a bar in Union Bridge where, sometimes in the evenings, he, my grandfather and the other men of my family would go to drink. Quite matter of factly, my uncle said: "Of course, we weren't allowed to sit up front with the white folks." Instead, the strong menfolks of my clan had to drink in the basement next to the furnace.

Imagine eagles being consigned to a basement! But that's how it was back then. The trick was that those eagles, even with their wings clipped by societal convention, managed nonetheless to fill their young eagles' heads with the notion that we could fly.

Today I celebrate the eagles in my life. I cry aloud for those who have flown from the nest, never to return again. And I clap hands and shout alleluia and amen for all the eagles who are still around.

I don't have the power to reconstruct the warmth and security of my early life in the nest. But on this Thanksgiving Day I thank God for having placed eagles all around me who fitted me with wings. On this day, I will fall to my knees and talk to the eagles wherever they are. I will tell them that their living was not in vain. I will tell all my eagles that they live on and on inside of me.

– *November 23, 1995*

Sweet as brown sugar

"Listen to your father, without him you would not exist . . ."

– Proverbs 22:25

George Washington Winston was born July 18, 1924, in Henrico County, Va. He joined the great black south-to-north migration, and by the early 1940s, George, whom childhood pals affectionately called Pungee, was happily living in Harlem.

Daddy told wonderful Harlem stories about the Apollo, stomping at the Savoy, the nightclubs, Father Divine's restaurants, and how on Seventh Avenue every Sunday was Easter Sunday, with men and women strutting, dressed to the nines.

My father made Harlem sound like Oz, complete with a yellow brick road, munchkins and wizards on every corner.

I imagine every little girl feels about her father like I did about mine. To me, Daddy was the most handsome, strongest and smartest man in the whole wide world. Nobody could beat Daddy, not even his hero, Joe Louis.

I loved my father, and I know that he loved me unequivocally.

Daddy was sugar cane; more specifically, he was brown sugar. And to him, I was at various times, his "Boopie Girl," his "papoose," his "Nooksie."

When I think of Daddy, I think brown. That color looked so good on him; it matched his smooth, dark chocolate complexion and his wavy hair.

So when Daddy died on Father's Day in 1983, there was no debate. We buried him in a brown suit in a brown, satin-lined coffin. And for a special touch, we took Daddy back uptown to Harlem.

*   *   *

When she found out who we were, the nurse at Byrd S. Coler Hospital said, "Your father died like a saint."

My sister Debbie and I had come to claim Daddy's belongings. The nurse couldn't have imagined how we, two of Daddy's three daughters, needed to hear that-to be uplifted in our grief. Perhaps she did know because cancer isn't a pretty disease.

It raged through my father's body for two and a half years, which was two years longer than the initial prognosis. The cancer, and the radiation and chemotherapy, stripped Daddy of a most cherished possession, his dignity.

So what could the nurse have been talking about?

Everything that I saw suggested that to me that, in his final days, all dignity was gone. My father controlled nothing, not even his basic bodily functions. I was a witness to his humiliation; he had to rely on others to take him to the bathroom and to give him an aspirin or drink of water. And if we weren't around or his caregivers were busy elsewhere, or simply weren't feeling particularly compassionate for a dying man, my father just had to wait.

Cancer had laid my father low. I often wondered, as I did 13 years later when my mother was dying of the same disease, what Daddy was thinking as he lain saying nothing, with a single tear snaking down his cheek.

That's what made the nurse's story seem so incredible.

No one was quite sure how Daddy managed it, but the nurse said that he got out of bed, maneuvered his frail 5-foot-9-inch frame into a wheelchair and rolled himself to the bathroom; this from someone who the day before couldn't even sit up. Daddy apparently washed his own face, combed his hair, and then wheeled himself back to his room. But once there, he was too weak to get himself back into the bed.

My father had dwindled to a featherweight, and the nurse was able without any assistance to lift him out of the wheelchair. Her intention was to put him back to bed. She said that when she gathered him up into her arms, he placed his head on her chest, took a deep breath and died.

"Like a saint," she said soothingly.

Now what the nurse couldn't have possibly have known simply by looking at the 59-year-old man in the hospital bed is that my father had always been meticulous about his appearance. Matter of fact, Daddy believed himself to be quite good-looking, and I agreed.

To be sure, my father, a minimum-wage laborer whose last job was pushing racks of clothes through New York's teeming Garment Center, didn't have expensive clothes; he couldn't afford them, not with three kids and a wife to feed. But what he had, Daddy kept cleaned and pressed.

So yes, I could imagine my father washing his face and combing his hair one last time; not wanting to meet his Maker looking any old kind of way.

But as sick and weak as he was, it was difficult believing that Daddy had died so easily. Despite my doubts, I wanted to believe that God had fixed it so that my brown-sugar Daddy would, like a sugar lump in hot water, simply melt away.

The proof would come later.

I was digging into the plastic hospital bag containing my father's personal effects. There were some papers and a small transistor radio. While rummaging in the bag my hand ran across something damp, and when I pulled it out, it was Daddy's face cloth.

It was all balled up, and incredibly, was still slightly wet even though my father had been dead two or three days.

God had sent the sign that I needed. And even now, my family is comforted by the nurse's story.

In his dying moments, Daddy, who was no angel, may have been touched by one.

He wasn't a churchgoer, and frankly, I don't recall my father talking much about God. The only thing he said was that when he was a boy in Virginia, a kind white lady he ran errands for paid his tuition to a Catholic school, where he completed the seventh grade, the end of his formal education.

But what I do know is that my father said his prayers nightly, even when he had been drinking. What's more, Daddy prayed the old-fashioned way. He'd get down on his knees, clasp his hands, rest his elbows on the mattress, close his eyes and recite, "Now I lay me down to sleep. I pray the Lord my soul to keep. If I should die before I wake, pray the Lord my soul to take."

Obviously, someone, my grandmother perhaps, taught my father that prayer when he was a small child, and he never wavered, and never stopped praying in that very same fashion.

So I know that my father was a believer, and I figure that God performed a miracle. Maybe God did for my father in his eleventh hour what Jesus did for Lazarus. Maybe God raised Daddy up one last time; restored my father's dignity one last time.

Mama always said that my father's life had been difficult. He lost both parents and the sight in one eye before he was 10 years old, and he was so poor that he sometimes had to wear women's clothes and shoes.

By comparison, my mother's life growing up in a big family in Maryland was heaven. That's why my mother constantly encouraged Debbie, Georgeann and me to cut Daddy a little slack.

My father had faults, plenty of them-who doesn't. And he and I would tangle when I'd do things he didn't approve of, such as stay out past curfew or go wandering off down by the East River Drive with some boy.

But, as strict as my father was, there's one thing my sisters and I never doubted: Daddy loved us and, if he had to, he would have died for us. I guess that's why, though my father is long gone, buried alongside my mother in Fair Lawn, N.J., I still do things that I hope will please him.

When the world looked at my father, I imagined it could see just another poor, black man, an alcoholic. But to me my father was brown sugar, as sweet as any father could be. And the scripture I'd choose to best describe my Dad is Psalms 118:22: "The stone which the builders rejected as worthless turned out to be the most important of all."

My father was larger than a stone. He was my rock.

– 2000

Mama used to say

A WHILE BACK, I was telling my Uncle Lonnie how much I miss my mother. He commiserated, saying, "I know. I miss my mother, too."

But how could that be? My father's younger brother was just 3 when their mother died in 1933.

Yet I didn't press my uncle. I was struck, however, by what I heard in Uncle Lonnie's voice. To think, not even the passage of 64 years has dimmed his yearning for a mother he knew just briefly.

Then it hit me. It's unnatural not to have one's mother. Many people, of course, go through life motherless and do just fine.

Still, for a great number, feelings of angst apparently never subside.

How blessed, therefore, I am to have had my mother for so many years. And more so to have had the type of mother that I did-a capable, compassionate, wise and sacrificing woman who often said, "If you're not willing to sacrifice, you shouldn't have children."

Now as I confront my first Mother's Day without her, I can't help but reflect on how often I feast upon my mother's words-her pithy one-liners that I often quote.

It is, however, somewhat disconcerting to grow up and realize that other people's mothers were telling them many of the same things.

page 29

How can that be?

Because there is, I'm convinced, something I call "Motherhood University."

Sadly, not all mothers graduate or even attend. Not all mothers have that mother wit. I'm talking about a mother's facility, through lessons and anecdotes, to instruct her children on ways to get from point A to point B without too much unnecessary stress.

Mother Sayings are intergenerational and universal. This was quickly evident when I solicited sayings from relatives, friends and colleagues who've grown up in different parts of the country and are of different ages, races and religions.

The repetition is astonishing. Also amazing is how much knowledge many mothers pack into few words. Indeed, some mothers don't need words, relying instead on gestures, looks and sighs to get their messages across.

Obviously, many Mother Sayings are religious in nature. I am convinced that the sayings on my list will bring to many readers' minds their own mothers' voices saying such things as:

* When friends all desert you, God won't.
* Play with fire, and you'll get burned.
* Lie down with dogs, and you'll get up with fleas.
* No means no!
* Keep it up. I'll give you something to cry for.
* You're getting too big for your britches.
* Your eyes are bigger than your stomach.
* People who live in glass houses shouldn't throw stones.
* Everybody you step on on the way up the ladder are people you'll run into on your way back down.
* Pretty is as pretty does.
* A woman always needs money she can call her own.
* As long as you're under my roof, you'll do as I say.
* Don't let me have to come up there!
* You can't make a silk purse out of a sow's ear.
* Don't marry a man without praying on it first.
* Keep your dress down!
* Keep your pants zipped!

* A man won't buy the cow if he can get the milk for free.
* An idle mind is the devil's workshop.
* A little hard work won't kill you.
* Kill your enemies with kindness.
* You can fool some of the people some of the time but not all of the people all of the time.
* There are no bad experiences, only good lessons.
* You can't judge a book by its cover.
* Children should be seen and not heard.
* Never let your bra strap show.
* Put on clean underwear. There may be an emergency that'll send you to the hospital.
* Nothing beats a try but a failure.
* Make your bed hard and you'll have to lie in it.
* The bigger they are, the harder they fall.
* Every dog has its day.
* I brought you into the world, I'll take you out.
* Never write a check that your behind can't cash.
* The apple doesn't fall far from the tree.
* It takes one to know one.
* Trouble doesn't last always.
* You'll learn!
* I can show you better than I can tell you.
* Always be bigger than the situation.
* You can take the people out of the country, but you can't take the country out of the people.
* Nothing stays the same.
* You can judge a person by the company she keeps.
* A good run beats a bad stand.
* If sense was so common, everyone would have it.

My mother said many of these things to my two sisters and me many times over.

But of all Mommy's Mother Sayings, the one I resisted hearing was, "Mama won't be here always."

– May 8, 1997

Products of our pasts

AFTER MONTHS of promises, two female friends and I made time to talk. The result was a marathon conversation that dredged up emotions ranging from laughter to rage.

At one point we talked about how it hurts to discover that a friend really isn't a friend at all. That part of the conversation left me wondering whether I'll ever graduate from Betty Brown Winston's School of Life. For years Mommy has been trying to teach me that a sure way to avoid the emotional sneak attacks that get me down is to "study" people.

"Don't listen to what they say, watch their eyes," Headmistress Mommy says.

"Since the eyes are the windows to the soul, they convey messages that often are opposite of an engaged mouth."

I found my long lunch with my friends refreshing for many reasons, especially the absence of the judgmental overtones that often pervade conversations when participants believe they know everything about one another.

One of Mommy's mottos is "Never tell anybody all about yourself, not your husband or your children, because you're liable to hear it again when it'll hurt."

Anyway, as my friends and I talked, I was reminded of how each of us has been shaped by our pasts. Each of us has been fashioned by the sweet and cruel things said and done to us throughout the years.

page 32

How foolish I often think it is for us to perceive ourselves as individuals; possibly even as unique. In fact, I'm amazed at how utterly un-unique we are. Just think. While we differ externally, we all have essentially the same operating parts inside.

What's more, like it or not, we're all shaped by forces beyond our control: by events that happened before our births; by people we'll never know; by chance encounters that technically would seem to have little to do with us.

And our life choices, I'd argue, aren't nearly as independent or as unpredictable as we're inclined to believe. Evidence abounds that our pasts profoundly impact our futures.

Clearly, my parents' pasts impacted how they raised me and my two sisters.

And that has impacted how my sisters are raising their children and is likely to impact how my nieces and nephew will raise theirs.

And so it goes.

In a roundabout fashion, this brings me to the troubling case of Shanda Renee Sharer, the 12-year-old Southern Indiana girl who was brutally murdered.

In recent weeks, this little corner of the world has been rocked and shocked by the cruelty of the four teenage girls who lured Shanda from her father's home on the pretext of a good time and then, in varying ways, participated in her death.

Shanda was choked. She was beaten with fists and instruments. She was sexually abused with a tire iron. And after hours of driving poor Shanda around in the trunk of a car, at least two of the girls doused their victim, who was still alive, with gasoline and set her on fire. They left the child to die in an Indiana field.

What manner of evil was that? What could make young girls hate so hard? What would make them mutilate Shanda so that her mother would say in court that they left her only child with "no face" and "so mutilated you couldn't tell she was a human being."

It occurred to me that the main motive for Shanda's death lies buried in the past: the pasts of the troubled teens who killed the child and the troubled pasts of the parents of the teens who killed Shanda.

Officially, though, the motive was jealousy: Melinda Loveless was angry over Shanda's friendship with 17-year-old Melinda's lesbian lover, 15-year- old Amanda Heavrin.

"Shanda would go up to the teacher's desk and Amanda would be staring at her. I'd see her and Amanda laughing and passing notes and I'd get mad," Loveless said.

A clinical psychologist said that 18-year-old Mary Laurine Tackett, who along with Melinda has been sentenced to 60 years in prison for Shanda's murder, has "no sense of self." Young Laurie's past, the psychologist said, is so negative that her experiences have dulled her pain, leaving her "incapable of feeling empathy for others."

Laurie's attorney, Ellen O'Conner, put it another way: "The public looks at this as a murder and asks how it could have happened. Clearly, these are not normal children. They come from dysfunctional homes. People say that's not an excuse. Well, it's not an excuse. It's an explanation."

And so it is.

This murder, and probably most murders, most rapes, and most instances of child and spouse abuse and other anti-social behavior, are the predictable results of the past-the ghosts that stalk many people, invading their presents and clouding their futures.

One of the poignant moments in the hearings was Laurie Tackett's assertion that she doesn't have "any memories of sunny days." But when I think about my two friends and me, it occurs to me that what got us through the sad times and the rough times was that we each had many, many sunny days.

And while many parents cannot give their children money, fine clothes or a grand house to live in, it's up to every parent to give their children sunny days. If not, their futures are predictable.

– *January 7, 1993*

Embracing the many good men

MY FATHER came to mind Sunday during my church's Men's Day celebration. I recalled what a fine man my father was and how terribly much I miss him.

George Winston wasn't perfect, but most who knew him will recall his generosity, pride in his family and patriotism. He never got over not being allowed to enlist during World War II because he was blind in one eye.

I looked up to and respected my father. I believed in him so much that I never doubted that, when he went off to work in the morning, he would come home that night.

He set the standard for how I define manhood. A true man is not judged by his physical strength, his age, his looks, or his job. My father showed me that a man is not ashamed to bow down on his knees every night to pray. He showed me that a man, even if deep down he's a little fearful, makes others in his household feel safe. A man deals with the inevitable disappointments in his life and doesn't use them as excuses not to keep on pushing.

My father showed me that a man can comfort a daughter who's made some mistakes and not say, "I told you so." One look is enough.

Page 35

Through my father's suffering, I discovered that a man need not lose faith and curse God because he, and not the guy down the street, has been diagnosed as having cancer.

Remembrances of my father and the void I feel because of his physical absence are what got me up out of my seat and onto my feet Sunday when those 100 men marched through the doors of St. Stephen Baptist Church and began singing. They were doing something positive, and it was a beautiful sight to see. It was a joy as well to be baptized in the blending of their voices- tenors, basses and baritones- displaying harmony far larger than the music.

These men came from all walks of life and from all sorts of circumstances.

No doubt, many weren't always candidates for sainthood, and they've probably done things in their lives that, if they could, they would do differently.

But on this Sunday, they stood tall, unified. They were uncuffed, unstooped, and unbowed by drugs or alcohol. There were 100 black men smiling and being free.

Men's Day and Women's Day are important observances in many African-American churches. Activities vary, but highlights invariably revolve around soul-stirring sermons, communal feasts, and singing unmatched on Broadway or at the Met. Increasingly the days are thematically linked to explorations of how faith intersects with and informs one's actions when confronting the spiritual and secular challenges of our times.

Sadly, 100 African-American men in tune with themselves and the universe is not a sight many of us see often enough. It's a sight some have never seen, specifically those whose perceptions of black men have been shaped largely by myths and media. Those perceptions are fed by daily doses of news stories that show black men shuffling in and out of court in handcuffs. Or black men looking menacingly out of police mug shots. Or black men in music videos who sing lewd lyrics while cradling their genitals, supposedly to the delight of bevies of young women dressed up and acting like tramps.

It's not often enough that the public at-large gets to see all the good black men-the men many of us are proud to call dad, husband, uncle, son, cousin, boyfriend, fiance, pastor, colleague, classmate, frat brother, godson, supervisor, financial advisor, or just friend. The black man's media

image is a perfect example of the good guys finishing last. Unlike in the movies, when it comes to black men in the media, the outlaws always seem to win.

So good black men like the ones at my church-who hold the elevator door when you're running late, who drive the buses you ride work, who wait tables at your favorite restaurant, who do your taxes, who ran and caught a thief and returned your purse-deserve to be encouraged. Good black men should know that we know that they exist. They should know that they're also being watched and written about.

Ultimately, good black men should know that America, and especially black America, needs them.

– Oct. 6, 1994

Back home in Gotham

IT WAS a rainy afternoon in New York City. A pretty young brown woman with tons of brown braids careening down her back slipped under the open-air bus shelter.

Suddenly, a napkin fluttered to the ground. The woman made no effort to retrieve it. In fact, she acted as if the napkin hadn't slipped out of her hand. Captured, I stared as the heavy rain quickly turned the napkin into a small mass of white mush.

Ah, New York City. Who picks up trash off its streets except those paid to do so or someone mentally disturbed?

Watching the napkin disintegrate, I felt like a tourist. Perhaps if I still lived in New York, the sight of someone dropping trash and not bothering to pick it up wouldn't have so thoroughly disgusted me.

Wait a second, I thought. Can it be that after only 12 years I've become a stranger in my hometown?

I enjoy my reconstructed existence in Louisville. Were that not so, I'd have left long ago. But as sure as my name is Betty, my roots are deep between the cracks of New York City streets. No matter where I live, or even where

I'm eventually buried, I'll always be at least part-New Yorker.

page 38

I was born in Brooklyn, educated in New York's public schools and universities, Hunter College and Columbia. I've had four different addresses in the Bronx, and once I bought a car, I ventured to Queens and Staten Island too.

I've been mashed and cursed on subways getting to and from work, and New York cabbies long ago schooled me in the fine art of giving the finger to klutzes behind the wheel.

During my homegirl life, I've stuffed myself with West Indian peas and rice and have calmed my hunger with roti from Indian restaurants on Manhattan's West Side. I've seen James Brown at The Apollo and Tito Rodriguez at The Palladium. I've danced in the old Audubon Ballroom where Malcolm X was assassinated, and the late jazz bassist Charlie Mingus bought me a Coke at the old Five Spot in Greenwich Village.

I've battled traffic on the East River Drive, and I remember when it didn't cost $3.50 each way to cross city bridges.

I've shopped on Delancey Street, been under the boardwalk at Coney Island and up on some roofs. My collection of books by and about Africans and African Americans began modestly with purchases from the old Micheaux's bookstore on 125th Street. I've witnessed furious black culture debates in the backroom of the old Liberty House.

I'm old enough to have personally experienced such icons of African-American culture-Baraka, the real Last Poets and Sonia Sanchez. I've seen plays at the old New Lafayette, and for a time performed uptown with National Black Theater.

I've eaten fried chicken at Club Lido and short ribs at LaFamile, and I remember when Sylvia's now-famous soul food restaurant on Lenox was nothing but a counter and a couple of booths.

I've had my Afro trimmed at the Shalimar, and I flirted with boys at the old boat house at the top edge of Central Park.

Recently, after seeing August Wilson's play, "Seven Guitars," I walked down Broadway and was reminded that the real drama is on New York City's streets.

Where else would a tall black man wearing sunglasses and ripped pants turn a piece of cardboard into a stage and dance like James Brown and then freeze until another passersby dropped coins into his cup?

I love the Big Apple. That's why I was so disturbed that a pretty young woman would drop her trash on the ground and act as if it was no big deal.

In years past, I might have tapped that young lady on the shoulder and said, "My dear, pick that up!" But I've not been gone from New York so long that I don't remember how such a gentle request, pretty woman or not, or even rushing to pick up the napkin myself, might have provoked a stream of curses or even a fight.

So I kept my mouth shut, allowing my disgust to remain lodged in my mind.

It's sad that many of us, whether we're in New York or wherever we live, just don't want to hassle.

– June 27, 1996

In the shadow of a bridge

THE WILLIAMSBURG BRIDGE is one of several over New York City's East River that connects Manhattan to Brooklyn, and one street the bridge crosses is Pitt. I lived there as a child in the shadow of the bridge.

Under the Williamsburg, where Delancey and Pitt streets intersect, there was a chicken market. Feathers were always flying as clucking birds fought for breathing room inside wooden crates stacked high.

Pitt Street stretches through lower Manhattan, but on our one block, there was P.S. 4, my elementary school; a synagogue; a candy store; a grocery store; a fruit and vegetable store; several apartment houses, and Anna'sBar.

Zoning apparently wasn't an issue, and all peacefully co-existed.

Children met at play and in school. Anna's was the place the grown folks went to sip, gossip, play the jukebox and dance. They loved Fats Domino, Johnny Ace, Clyde McPhatter and Ruth Brown.I know because sometimes my father took me into Anna's, and then bribed me with pretzels from the bar not to tell my mother that I had been there.

Also on Pitt, closer to Houston, was Pitt Street Park. Mommy warned me, "Nooksie, don't go into the sprinklers." I went anyway, and while I was getting wet, somebody stole my shoes!

"Ooooh, yo' Mama's gonna git you," my friends chanted, and I cried, knowing that they were right.

"Didn't I [swat!] tell you [swat!] not to [swat!] . . ." my mother said in Mama cadence while spanking my bottom all the way home.

A new pair of shoes was an unwelcome expense for poor people.

I lived on Pitt until fourth grade. My family lived in two buildings on the block, 57 and 60 Pitt Street, the latter of which actually had a name.

"Alma" was carved into the stone. I don't know who Alma was or how she rated having a building named after her, but Aunt Catherine always threatened to write a book about 60 Pitt and name the book "Alma" after our building.

Pitt Street was typical New York City in the 1940s and '50s. Peddlers ambled through selling ice, fish, eggs, fruit and even rags.

A less fond Pitt Street memory is of the big-as-cats rats that trolled the hallways, cellars and vacant lots. The nasty things were lured no doubt by the bags of garbage that people "air mailed" out their windows.

Pitt Street had many memorable human characters, people such as Zula; Miss Ola; Miss Ethel; WeeWee; Neal, the blind man; and Nat, who though black, had adopted a Jewish accent.

"So, whatsamatter for you?" Nat would say.

There was the old Jewish lady who lived in 60 Pitt and who couldn't pronounce Nooksie. So when she'd see me running up the steps, she'd say, "Ritzy! Ritzy! Where are you going so fast?"

Then there was Dove. He loved me. Sometimes he dressed in women's clothes, and he was known to pester women neighbors to "borrow" Kotex. Dove once claimed to be pregnant, causing my father to fall down laughing. But Dove was serious, my mother said.

At its heart, Pitt Street was home to a collection of strivers from abroad and down South.

My memories of life on the street came roaring back recently, the day a madman shot up the Jewish Community Center in Los Angeles and wounded a teenager, an elderly woman and several children.

I guess it's because one of my best friends on Pitt Street was a little Jewish girl named Deborah. I loved her so much that I got my mother to name my little sister Deborah.

When I heard about the L.A. rampage, I remembered Deborah and thought that the children who were in harm's way could have been her grandchildren. I wondered how someone whose mother was a Holocaust survivor reacts to anti-semitism so virulent that it provokes a madman to shoot at babies.

I never saw Deborah again after we moved from Pitt Street in 1955. But all these years later, she's my spiritual connection to a terrible crime.

The L.A. Jewish Community Center shootings speak to me of vulnerability, and in particular, how vulnerable we people of color, like Jews, are to white supremacists.

When you live inside these skins, you try not to think about it all the time. But you are constantly aware that while this time it was the Jewish Community Center in L.A., tomorrow the terror easily might be visited upon the places where our children go to play and to learn.

Meanwhile, it's doubtful that I'll ever run across my friend Deborah again.

But I do remember her. I remember her synagogue and her mother's wigs and tattoos.

And if I should ever encounter Deborah again, I believe I'd throw open my arms, pull her inside and whisper, "I've never forgotten."

– *August 26, 1999*

Life: A risky business

NIGHT HAD FALLEN. As I gathered up my things and prepared to conclude a visit with my friend Fredericka Teer, I fretted about how I'd safely navigate the dimly lit streets from her Manhattan apartment to the subway a few blocks away.

When I told Fredericka about my skittishness, she said that I must not live in fear of my environment. She said that if I intended to live in New York as opposed to simply exist there, I had to live with my environment. There stood Illinois native Fredericka giving me a lecture on how to live in my hometown.

But Fredericka could talk. Back then, I'd never lived outside New York.

Fredericka had lived on the East Coast, the West Coast, places in between, and abroad. I was impressed by Fredericka's fearlessness and how she, seemingly with no effort, could sculpt order from chaos.

Fredericka, who died of natural causes in 1973, seemed to engage life rather than simply letting life engage her. She seemed to appreciate and embrace life's beauty, while at the same time seeking to understand its challenges and contradictions.

I thought about Fredericka when reading about last month's terrorist bombing at New York City's World Trade Center in which five people were killed and more than a thousand were injured.

I wondered what Fredericka's response would have been to the World Trade Center survivor who vowed never to set foot in the twin towers again.

The Courier-Journal editorialized that the terrorist bombing was a chilling reminder of what people in such places as Beirut, Bogota and Belfast long have lived with. "No one is immune to terrorism," the editorial said. "We are all potential prey to random acts of violence, and on some gut level, we're all afraid."

I can imagine Fredericka reading the editorial, contemplating its meaning, and then, in her soft-spoken way, asking: "But what are we to do with our fears?"

Fears are real.

I've tried to confront many of mine. Some I've conquered simply through experience. Yet, some fears stalk and gnaw at the edges of my consciousness even when outwardly I'm cool, calm and collected.

For example, when I'm riding in an airplane bouncing through turbulent skies, I'm painfully reminded that, though I travel often, I've not truly conquered my fear of flying. When I'm in an airplane, there's the nagging reality that I am not in control.

I haven't lived in New York for nearly a decade. And when I go home to visit, I find myself less fearful than vigilant, much more vigilant than when I'm back in Kentucky.

When I'm in New York, I consciously try not to look like a victim by the city's standards. Depending on where I am in the city, I adopt a certain swagger, a certain I-dare-you stare. Occasionally, I strategically place my hand inside my coat pocket as if I'm armed.

But as the World Trade Center bombing reminds, vigilance, indeed the keenest of awareness, often offers little or no protection from some real dangers.

Take, for example, Sept. 14, 1989. That was the day I arrived at work and, for hours, wasn't permitted inside the building because a massacre had occurred shortly before my arrival.

Had I come to work a few minutes earlier, I could have been in the building when Joseph Wesbecker was on his shooting spree. Wesbecker, a former pressman at Standard Gravure Corp., the building then adjacent to *The Courier-Journal*, had gone berserk, and had shot 20 people, apparently at random. Eight people died.

In a very short time, a man with psychological problems, an AK-47 semiautomatic rifle and a 9-mm. handgun had rocked our safe little world in Louisville.

I suppose many of us newspaper and Standard Gravure employees could have decided that, like that World Trade Center worker, we'd never again set foot

back inside the building. But such a decision would only have meant that we were surrendering our lives and our livelihoods to a person many of us didn't know, and who, by his own hand, was already dead.

Not ever coming back into the newspaper building, I imagine, would have given some people a sense of security. To me, however, it would have been a false sense that life isn't what I think life really is: a crap shoot.

Fredericka, I've decided, was right to force me to think about whether I wished fear to rule my life. I believe she was right to remind me that there's no way really for us live and shield ourselves from all dangers, particularly the dangers we often aren't aware exist.

So when the all-clear is given, I think most of the thousands who work or do business in the World Trade Center will return to their stations. That's what we in Louisville had to do after Wesbecker turned what started out as a routine workday into a horror we'll never will forget.

Most people who've survived some tragedy are forever changed. Usually, they're chastened by such experiences.

But such experiences ought to do something more. They should remind us that living is risky business, and that more often than not, the odds appear in our favor.

– March 11, 1993

Chapter Four:

Sage

Remembering the mythology of goodness

THE FACE of the light-complexioned redhead on the front page of the newspaper was awfully familiar.

Neoma Clark and I lived a few miles apart. Maybe we crossed paths in the supermarket aisles. Maybe we met at church, the beauty shop, or a gathering of women. Maybe I never actually met Neoma Clark but remember her from the news story when she became only the second African-American woman inducted into the Louisville Softball Hall of Fame.

Unfortunately, if I never met Neoma Clark, I'll never get the chance.

Firefighters found the charred remains of the 50-year-old softball fanatic smoldering in a bedroom of her West Louisville home. Clark, a secretary, had been strangled and set afire.

She died wearing her softball uniform. She had taken the day off from work to prepare for the Charmettes' trip to Michigan to compete in the Black World Softball Tournament.

Hours after Clark's body was discovered, her 27-year-old son, Larry Fulton White Jr., was arrested. He is charged with murdering his mother and setting the fire to cover up the evil deed. His motive? He was upset with his mother, who was imploring him to find steady work.

Sons have killed their mothers before. Yet, many African Americans grew up believing our people did not commit this kind of crime.

It once was common for black elders to instruct youths like this: "We may be poor. We may not be educated. And we may be despised because we're black, but our people don't commit suicide. We don't put our babies up for adoption. We don't put our old people in nursing homes against their will."

The elders acknowledged that some black people gambled, got drunk and raised hell on the weekend. Then they would wag their fingers, straighten their backs and say with great pride: "But we don't commit mass murder. We don't abuse our kids. And we don't kill the whole family because one of us has had a bad day."

Wise children didn't challenge the elders, didn't demand proof that what they said was true and not merely wishful thinking.

Frankly, in our black world, there seemed to be sufficient evidence to back up those assertions. It was rare to hear of a black person committing suicide, killing a parent or giving a baby up for adoption by strangers. A child whose biological parents weren't up to raising him was passed on to relatives or to close family friends.

Once grown, African Americans steeped in what a psychologist might describe as the mythology of the inherent goodness of the oppressed, understood that the elders' motive was to swell our pride in what we were, who we were, and where we came from.

By passing down the mythology, the elders were trying to equip us with the moral defenses they knew we would need in a hostile world, where we'd likely be inundated with more negatives about ourselves than positives.

By instructing us that our people were more righteous and more moral than our oppressors, black elders were conveying a code of conscientiousness. The Christian ones intended to assure young African Americans that despite our condition, the Creator loved us and mercifully had given us virtues that our oppressors lacked.

The mythology of our goodness was the balm that cooled our wounds. It was the salve that soothed our souls when hostile teachers, misguided preachers, sociologists and others said that black people were nothing, came from nothing, and wouldn't amount to anything-no matter how hard we tried.

African Americans baptized in the mythology of our goodness are sickened any time one of our own is accused of some heinous act we were told black people do not commit.

Old-school African Americans ask what people have come to when Rosa Parks, the mother of the civil rights movement, now in her 80s, gets beaten and robbed in her home. Parks' attacker must not have been listening when his elders recited the litany of things black people don't do. The man who attacked Rosa Parks didn't care or know that she a heroine. On that night, she was a target: a helpless, old black woman at home alone.

It's been said of late that these are the best and the worst of times for African Americans. Many have come pretty far pretty fast since the days when our skin color restricted where we could live, work, eat, shop, play, go to the bathroom or attend school. Many older African Americans are both proud of and astonished by our progress.

Yet their eyes run water when they realize that they've lived long enough to see some of us make liars of our elders by committing acts of terrorism that our ancestors were so proud of saying black people never did.

Black elders often ask what's the true price of all this alleged progress.

Have some of us gained the world, but lost our souls?

– September 15, 1994

Heroes in sports, absentee dads in life

ONE DAY when he was a youngster in the South Bronx, my former husband encountered his father on the street. He hadn't seen his father in a while, so he filled him in on what was going on in his life.

As the conversation ended, he told his father that he needed a new pair of shoes. His dad patted his head and said as he walked away, "So do I, son. So do I."

Often, after we were divorced, I wondered if my husband's lack of a secure, loving relationship with his dad was the ghost that had haunted our marriage.

Having once loved a neglected, rejected son, I was eager to read the recent *Sports Illustrated* article about pro athletes who've fathered children, often out of wedlock, and have not been there for those children emotionally.

My former husband's father was a boxer from the Dominican Republic.

Sports Illustrated's cover featured Khalid Minor, the beautiful son of Boston Celtics guard Greg Minor. The child is holding a basketball, and superimposed over his photo is the headline "Where's Daddy?"

Being no stranger to the myths and stereotypes about black male sexuality, I took a deep breath before I opened the magazine. Most of the pros who figure prominently in SI's absent daddy hall of shame are black. But other players, including

page 50

former Celtic star Larry Bird, hockey's Mark Messier, baseball's Juan Gonzalez and boxer Oscar De La Hoya, are inductees too.

The article reports that the never-married basketball star Shawn Kemp has seven children by at least five women. New England Patriots running back Dave Meggett is said to have had four out-of-wedlock children by three women.

The article also says, however, that nearly a dozen attorneys who have handled such cases say that 90 percent of the paternity suits against pro athletes never get into the public record because they're settled quietly.

In other words, no one can really say how many such children there are or how many pro athletes are out-of-wedlock fathers.

Of course, as SI noted, there are paternity claims against the pros that turn out to be false. What's more, they're nothing new. Apparently, what is new now that the average NBA salary is $2.2 million is that players can end up having to pay astronomical sums for their romps between the sheets-sometimes to women they barely know.

The tale *Sports Illustrated* weaves isn't pretty. But after reading it, I considered the profound lessons that readers were supposed to take away.

I'm not shocked, for example, that there are women who chase pro athletes down in search of a payday.

Was I just outdone to learn that many of the pro players initially denied paternity? I wasn't.

I'm also not shocked that Magic Johnson's poignant appeals after his HIV diagnosis apparently have fallen on so many deaf ears.

The fact is, when it comes to money and fame, it isn't news any more that for some people, nothing is sacred. It's not an explosive revelation that for the sake of bragging rights, or a few moments of intimacy with a rich, famous man or with a pretty woman, some people are willing to risk everything, including their lives.

Unprotected sex between two consenting adults is one thing. It is quite another to put a child's life at risk, either physically or emotionally.

I'm no prude. But what would motivate the mother of one of Shawn Kemp's children, after he told her he had children by five other women that he didn't marry, to join that club? Love? Money? What?

Frankly, I found few heroes in the *Sports Illustrated* article but more than enough victims to go around. The children are the primary victims, even if mom is collecting $7,000 a month in a child support.

But there are other victims, too. They're not obvious now, but they'll start to mount up when some of these children who are now being neglected or rejected by their fathers grow up, try to establish intimate relationships of their own, only to discover that there's a nasty ghost in the closet.

– May 14, 1998

An eye-opening week as a 'mom'

LIKE MANY childless women, I like to believe that if I had a child, I'd be a perfect mother.

I'd always in the mood to listen to my child's concerns and would have at the ready profound answers for the profound questions children often ask.

I'd cook like Betty Crocker, keep my home immaculate and cheerfully volunteer for the PTA.

I got my chance to play Mommy when 15-year-old Zandilé came to visit.

I first met Zandilé when she was 8. Her father, Kabral Blay Amihere, a distinguished African journalist, and I were Nieman Fellows at Harvard University. Like many Niemans, Kabral brought his family to Cambridge, Mass.

As I had no children, I believe that the dozen or so "Nieman kids" that year, including Zandilé and her younger sister, Zeba, came to think of me as something of an Auntie Mame, part clown, part eccentric.

Zandilé was a beautiful and loving child, and we kept in touch. Still, it surprised me when she called and asked to come to Louisville for a visit.

No sooner had I said yes than I began to fret about how I, the ultimate single woman, might keep a teenager entertained for a week or more. And what if 15-year-old Zandile was not the sweet child that I knew in Cambridge?

I pressed friends for ideas about how I could make Zandilé's visit a wonderful experience.

page 53

"You'll do fine; kids love you," said one sympathetic friend.

Eventually, I had a plan. I'd enroll Zandilé in my church's summer program during my working hours, and during my free time, I'd squire her around to a few local attractions.

Piece of cake, I figured.

But then crisis struck: I couldn't meet Zandilé at the airport. My friend agreed to pick her up. I described him in detail to Zandilé. The last thing I needed was for some stranger to walk off with her, necessitating my having to call her mother, Ama, and say, "I've misplaced your daughter."

Crisis averted, I was pleased to see that Zandilé has blossomed into a stunning young adult; she's mannerly and personable. "Thank you, Jesus!" I said to myself several times.

Also to my absolute delight, like her father, mother and me, Zandilé has journalism in her genes. She writes well, and come fall, she'll be editor in chief of her school newspaper in New Jersey.

And here I was worried that she'd be bored to death visiting with me at *The Courier-Journal*. Instead, she was anything but bored, charming many colleagues with her attentiveness. I felt like a proud parent and thought, yes, this could be my child.

I discovered, too, that she didn't need constant stimulation from me.

Indeed, Zandilé was perfectly content in her downtime to curl up and read a book while listening to Maxwell, whose music we mutually love.

I had to laugh the day that Zandilé pulled one of my books off the shelf, Thylias Moss' *Tale of a Sky Blue Dress*, a memoir about child abuse, read a few pages and then announced, "Auntie Betty, this is way over my head."

This is my child, I decided.

I never enrolled Zandilé in my church's summer program because once she met my pastor's daughter, Christine, they came up with their own agenda.

The two girls decided, for example, that Zandilé would

spend a night at Christine's house and that they and a couple of Christine's girlfriends would spend an afternoon hanging out at the amusement park. Then Christine invited Zandilé to her mother's family reunion in the Lexington area, and they decided that later in the week they'd go to the movies.

As Christine's mother, Barnetta, reminded me several times, teenagers don't need us hovering about.

I put Zandilé on the airplane early yesterday, and as I walked back to my car, I realized that this girl has yet again managed to crawl up into my heart-has managed to remind me of what fun it would be to have a daughter like her.

The time I spent with Zandilé this summer has increased my respect for relatives and friends I've watched over the years struggling, often alone, to raise their children.

I was reminded of how carefree my life must seem to those parents who don't take pleasure trips because their most important investments are in their children's futures.

As Zandilé's plane was climbing through the clouds, I realized anew the juggling acts most parents perform day in and day out to give their children a little more than the basics.

Having experienced Zandilé reminded me of how my friend Emma Talbott, a retired teacher and a parenting expert, often says that parents don't raise children single-handedly, but that children are influenced as well by the other adults in their lives.

One evening, Zandilé inched up beside me on the couch, hugged me, nuzzled my neck and said, "Auntie Betty, I love you." I melted. Matter of fact, I cried when I recalled all the times when I was about Zandilé's age, and I, too, would hug my mother and tell her that I loved her.

I didn't know, of course, most of the things my mother was going through.

But I must have been perceptive as Zandilé is, and I must have known instinctively that Mama could use a kiss, a hug and hearing that she was loved and appreciated.

– July 23, 1998

Breaking the silence

MICHELLE JOHNSON was terrified. "It was like standing up in front of my parents; standing up in front of my family."

Tom Morgan didn't expect a crowd early on a Saturday. "We had to order more chairs twice," he said. "I was absolutely thrilled that so many people were interested in this issue."

The issue was black gays and lesbians.

Never in the National Association of Black Journalists' 18-year history had its 2,000 or so members openly broached the subject of gays and lesbians among us.

And that's true even though in 1989, NABJ members elected Tom as our president.

We elected Tom, an editor at *The New York Times*, but other than nasty slurs during the campaign, Tom's homosexuality was rarely discussed.

Though some at the NABJ convention in Houston probably knew that Michelle, a copy editor at *The Boston Globe*, is a lesbian, most did not. Michelle, after all, doesn't wear a big L on her forehead.

"I had such anxiety," she said describing how she felt when she essentially "came out of the closet."

"But why?" I asked about that anxiety.

"Because you know black folks," Michelle said. "We can be tough on our own. You step outside the line and somebody whacks you upside your head. It's the tradition."

Page 56

Michelle didn't get whacked. But traditionally black people generally haven't discussed homosexuality – and would appreciate it if black gays and lesbians didn't talk about it either.

Our silence persists even though homosexuals are deeply woven into the fabric of our lives. It's an open secret that many of our black heroes and heroines were and are gay. But most also have kept silent, allowing themselves and us to focus exclusively on their achievements.

"They kept silent for the sake of the race," Tom said. "But for how long?"

Forever, I imagine many black people would say.

Right or wrong, many black people fear that the push for gay rights distracts from the struggle against racism. On the agenda of collective black suffering, some do not perceive gay rights as deserving to rank as high as racial discrimination, poverty, crime and other issues with which we struggle.

So former NABJ president and *Chicago Sun-Times* columnist Vernon Jarrett was speaking for many black people when he said he deeply resents gay activists, whether black or white, appropriating the language of the civil rights movement to make the case that homosexuals are as oppressed as black people.

He was heckled and booed, but Vernon didn't hold his tongue.

Predictably, many others did.

Indeed, it was more than ironic that black journalists, many of whom are outspoken on practically everything on NABJ's agenda, feared expressing an honest opinion lest we be perceived ignorant or worse, homophobic. Whites often approach matters of race in the same way, fearing the brand of racist.

I believe many were silent because they appreciated the seemingly inherent contradiction for black people to be publicly seen, even tacitly, as condoning the oppression of any minority group.

The speakers at the NABJ forum talked about the gay-bashing that goes on, and, they said, many of the victims have been black.

During the forum, I saw tears. I sensed in some people a longing for understanding. I also saw pain etched into the faces of a few of my colleagues. I realized that I hadn't noticed that pain before. I realized that perhaps I had never made my friends feel comfortable enough to know that if they wished, they could have told me that they were lesbian or gay.

And their pain continues to haunt. Hence this column. Hence my calling Tom and Michelle to ask the obvious: What is it that gay and lesbian journalists want from NABJ, and what is it that they want from me?

"I want NABJ members to just recognize the commonalities between the between the struggle for gay rights and black rights," Michelle said. "They are not exactly the same, but there are some common themes." One commonality, she said is workplace discrimination.

Tom doesn't expect NABJ or all people to embrace the gay agenda. Nonetheless, he said, black journalists who are straight, as professionals working in an important field, must avail themselves of information. They must, in fact, be educated about a part of black life that most of us know little about, he added.

And so the tables have turned. Now it's non-gay black journalists who must be educated, much in the way we have sought-with varying degrees of success-to educate our white media colleagues about the broader African-American experience.

Black journalists who do stories about gays, like whites who write about race, must force our way past stereotypes. It's only fair since we are in the image-making business.

"The media hasn't been looking for us," Tom said. "And that's like it is in the rest of society. Black gays and lesbians, like black people in general, have been marginalized."

- August 5, 1993

Facing one's own anti-gay bias

I HAVE SAID ugly things about gay people, and I've laughed at gay jokes.

I know firsthand the sting of contempt and how bigotry can suck the light right out of a person's world, and still I allowed negative utterances to fall from my lips.

Me, a homophobe!

But like racists, I comforted myself as not really being homophobic because I did and do have gay friends. I couldn't really be homophobic because I'd never stoop to physically attacking a gay person or marching in an anti-gay parade.

But I was homophobic. Looking back, I realize that I was no different from those whites who say that since they didn't invent racism they can't be held accountable for it or be expected to do anything meaningful about it.

Homophobia, like racism, is embedded in the culture; and bigotry doesn't die easily.

Growing up, I never heard the terms lesbian or gay. Instead, gay people were called sissies, punks, faggots, butches and dykes. I don't know the derivation of these terms, but I know that when uttered, they sounded and felt like hissing.

Even my father admonished my two sisters and me to stop smooching my nephews so much lest the boys grow

page 59

up, Daddy said, and become faggots instead of men.

I recall the occasion when my late husband, Brian, slammed some poor guy into a jukebox, saying, "He looked at me funny."

Such things still do happen, and they're the reasons why I often say that if there's anything I wouldn't ever want to be, it's gay, and especially not black and gay since, I'm sorry to say, many African Americans are rabidly homophobic.

Perhaps it's because African Americans have so much else to contend with that homosexuality on top of it all is just too much.

Whatever the reason, African Americans are a mass of contradictions relative to homosexuality. In our churches, for example, some of the same preachers who'll reduce you to tears with stirring, Biblically referenced denunciations of racism may in the next breathe thunder against homosexuals, as if gay men and lesbians aren't sitting in the choir and in the pews.

It's crazy, but many African-American Christians will shout to James Cleveland's gospel, yet deny what was an essential part of his being-that besides being a great singer and composer of religious music, Cleveland was also homosexual.

I was reminded of how hatred finds powerful allies in silence and excuses watching a 26-minute documentary, "All God's Children." The video was jointly sponsored by Woman Vision, the National Gay and Lesbian Task Force Policy Institute and the National Black Gay and Lesbian Leadership Forum.

The documentary evidences the black-on-black mistreatment of gays and lesbians. It documents how our ignorance and contempt have driven many homosexual brothers and sisters into "dark and lonely closets."

The Rev. Jesse Jackson appears in the documentary. "Whenever we begin to make these great judgments-about who is superior, who is inferior, who is chosen and who is the master, who is worthy, who is unworthy-the premise is then laid for violent attacks, for destruction and murder, and for harm and injury," Jackson said. "We must reject that. We are all God's children."

Also to the point in the powerful documentary is the Rev. Cecil L. Murray, pastor of the First A.M.E. Church in Los Angeles. The Rev. Murray says to African-American Christians, "After being excluded all of your life-after

knowing the stigma of being labeled and typed and stereotyped, and being treated as if you are an outside child of God-if that doesn't sensitize you to human beings as human beings, if that doesn't make you take the stand of the underdog, then you are a real dog."

Truly, I was already fired up by the time I met a small group of gay activists for dinner. Our group talked a lot about the stuff of life: politics, culture, religion, and Sen. Jesse Helms.

Mandy Carter, who was in Louisville to deliver the keynote address at a conference the following day, is a powerful woman. At last year's National Gay and Lesbian Task Force annual conference, she said that Helms was still in office because "the gay community couldn't get over its racism to work with (Democratic nominee Harvey) Gantt, and the black community couldn't get over its homophobia and work with us."

Of course, there are many others like Helms. They've thrived on the politics of hate and division among people who, if they could sit together and talk together, might just find that there is more common ground among us than we are led to believe. Failing to find that common ground never benefits the masses, only the few.

– *April 10, 1997*

Misguided TV guidance

THE AD on a cable music channel boldly suggested that the last thing a young person ought to wish for is to grow up to become like his or her parents.

I was so agitated that I said to myself that I was either getting very old or very old-fashioned. Surely some parents aren't great role models. Some parents aren't even very good human beings. Such people, however, do not constitute a majority.

Even as I deplored the TV ad, it occurred to me that I had finally become one of them: a member of the establishment.

Though I think of myself as progressive enough at least to consider what young people say they're saying in their music, their styles and attitudes, I'm increasingly forced to acknowledge that I am a product of my times.

Though some in my generation claimed no one over 30 could be trusted, I never believed that. No one ever could convince me that all grown-ups were untrustworthy, uninspiring and stupid. In fact, there were many people I really did want to be like when I grew up.

In the world my parents shaped for me, children were not considered little adults. Children had their place in the social order and were expected to remain there unless instructed by responsible adults to do otherwise.

Children generally did not have the unfettered access and right to comment on grown-up affairs. Those privileges came with age, wisdom and experience.

Indeed, it was this unwritten understanding that seemed to give most young people of my generation something to look forward to when we did grow up.

When I moved out of my parents' home at 17 after graduating from high school, I knew that there wasn't any dispute that in my parents' house, whether I was 17 or 71, I had to live by their rules. Those rules, by today's standards, probably would seem Draconian, if not abusive. In general, the rules were non-negotiable. What's more, the crimes and the punishments were clear.

Serious offenses like ignoring curfew or going where one was explicitly instructed never to be caught dead or alive drew the equivalent of home incarceration for whatever length of time my parents, not I, deemed fair.

Very serious offenses like skipping school, getting caught in a bald-faced lie, or doing anything with a boy in an elevator or up on the roof was punishable by the back of the hand plus house arrest.

When I committed a crime, there was no question that I would do the time.

So when I decided that I had grown up enough to stay out as long as I wished, wherever I wished, with whomever I wished, doing whatever I wished, I already knew that freedom wasn't free.

Emancipation, I had been told dozens of times, required me to pay my own bills and not to dare expect my parents, who were struggling to make it anyhow, to foot the expenses for my liberation.

The TV ad caused me to think about whether we've actually become better individuals or a better society now that the line between children and adults has been thoroughly blurred. Are we better off now that many young people believe it is perfectly OK, if not their sworn duty, to be consulted or to comment on anything and everything?

I don't wish to be trapped into claiming that everything was good about the good old days. It wasn't. Still, I'm amazed with what children, including pre-teens, now commonly get away with.

Young, unmarried girls wearing pregnancy as if it's some badge of honor.

Young boys routinely calling their girlfriends and their girlfriends' mothers bitches and whores. Those used to be fighting words.

I can't imagine, even now, what I'd face if my father flicked on his TV and saw me half-dressed and jiggling my breasts and behind on somebody's video.

I can't even picture myself, with my feet under my father's table, eating my father's food and wearing clothes he and my mother slaved to buy, informing them that it's my thing and they can't tell me who to sock it to.

It's clear that widespread parental permissiveness hasn't resulted in widespread parental respect. Indeed, it seems to have spawned disrespect, such as the commercial that tells young people to be anything except like their parents.

More parents and adults in positions to influence young people must assume adult postures, attitudes and responsibilities. More adults must set the agenda and the tone about what is and isn't going to be tolerated in our homes, at our schools, on our streets and in our neighborhoods.

Yes, I must be getting old. I'm convinced that if given more opportunities to interact with adults who act like adults – dispensing knowledge, discipline, and good reasons why families and societies must have rules – more children might be proud to grow up to be like us. If we assume our jobs as responsible adults, then ads like the one I saw either might never be made, or young people, en masse, might reject them.

– January 6, 1994

A miraculous journey from abuse

THE MINUTE I spied the return address on the envelope sticking out of my mailbox, I became excited. It's been at least 10 years since I saw Fatima.

We met at the National Black Theater in New York in the late 1960s. There, we didn't call ourselves actors, but liberators. Fatima and I were in our 20s. We were the original Fly Girls. We were militant and strong. It was black-power time, and Fatima and I were dead up in it.

We adopted African names, dressed in African-inspired attire, and, of course, wore our hair, which we sometimes wrapped in colorful cloth, au naturel. A letter from Fatima after all these years. How exciting!

But there was no letter inside the envelope. Inside were a couple of fliers trumpeting Fatima Johnson's book, *Fatima's Miraculous Journey*.

Great, I thought. Another writing friend is published. Hooray!

But Fatima's book is not fiction. It's not pretty. It's painful poetry about her life.

No. I can't, I don't want to believe that my beautiful, laughing friend was sexually molested by her father from the time she was 12 until she was 15. No way.

A trial? Fatima's father's lawyer portrays her as just a girl with a creative imagination. The jury isn't fooled. He's found guilty and serves seven years in prison.

But does he repent? No. He tries to molest Fatima again when she's in her 20s. But then she was grown and able to fight back.

All that just couldn't have happened to my friend. Why didn't she tell me?

We did spend lots of time together over several years. But Fatima, that girl, never said a word.

She told me on the phone the other night that victims often don't talk. One of the poems in her book, "What's It Like to be Angry? I Gotta Learn That" explains.

I had to push it down
and lock it up deep inside
if I was angry I couldn't show it
if I was sad, you'd better not know it.
What would I get for my tears, for my anger
The strap!
A smack!
A knock down!
Go to bed!

And here's a line from Fatima's poem/prayer: "Oh, God, deliver us from all the sex offenders of this world, especially those who touch little children in some violating way."

But what if Fatima had told me back in the Dark Ages, the 1960s? What would we have done with such information, living, as many of us were, in some Ozzie-and-Harriet dream? Even now, some say the painful and ugly things that happened to Fatima didn't really happen. Such happenings are instead symptoms of a newly troubled world, they say. We blissfully ignore the fact that not even Ozzie and Harriet ever really lived Ozzie-and-Harriet lives.

All those years ago at National Black Theater, Fatima was always writing. But when we talked the other night, she said she stopped for about 15 years.

Not until October 1993, "when I went into primal therapy," she said, "did the poems start coming again."

During what she terms her "healing flight from child abuse," Fatima says that she wrote 40 poems. One is called "Little Miss America? No, Saddest Little Girl of the Year."

Fatima instructs that this poem be sung rather than spoken. Its first stanza goes like this:

It's so sad
how unhappy one little 12-year-old girl can be.
Look at me and my smilin' face.
Pretty ain't it.
But you don't know what I go through inside
and the hell when the lives collide inside the house I live.

Fatima acknowledges that the poetry in her book is "raw." But then, so is child sexual abuse.

One of the poems was inspired by a news story Fatima read about a 4-year-old beaten to death by her parents. The child's spleen was busted, her liver shattered and she suffered contusions to the head. Fatima writes of how the child returns to her parents as a ghost, an angel really. She tells them to leave her brother and sister alone and never to have any other children because "We are watching you."

Fatima's Miraculous Journey is not a book for children. "It's a protest of the injustices done to children," Fatima said.

Today, my dear friend is 50 years old. Her two sons, Gregory and Chaka, are grown. Fatima is a doting mother-in-law and grandmother. And finally, through therapy, plus the support and encouragement of friends and family, Fatima is on the way to being healed.

"You have to talk about it, write about it, just get it out in some kind of way so that it's not self-destructive," she said.

Talking to Fatima about her suffering reminded me of something I occasionally forget: It's impossible for us to really know our friends unless our friends really want us to know them. The best that we can do when friends, through words or deeds, disappoint is remember that what's really at work may be factors beyond their control. What may be at work is pain that they've yet to come to terms with.

As for Fatima, I'm not worried about her. She'll be OK because, she said, "I feel like I'm still a liberator. I was excited about being a liberator. I feel like that's my mission in life."

– October 27, 1994

It's not easy in beautiful Ghana

GHANAIAN journalist Kabral Blay-Amihere and Philip Bunmi Aborisade, a Nigerian journalist-in-exile in Ghana, have a routine in which they look at each other, smile and say, "It's not easy." Those words are a pretty accurate description of how I found daily life during the three weeks I spent in the Republic of Ghana.

Matter of fact, I returned from West Africa determined never again to complain about hard work. Hard work is that done by Ghanian coal peddlers, whose days are spent bent over and sifting through mountains of black nuggets along the streets of Accra. Hard work is that done by Ghanaian market women too. Their hours of haggling produce stacks of Ghanaian currency, cedis, that are so devalued that at day's end there isn't much to speak of.

Hard work is rural women toting babies on their backs and water or stacks of firewood atop their heads. It's 13-year-old Ebenezer, of Tamale, who craves education so desperately that he leaves home at 4:30 a.m. to walk miles to school. Hard work is reaping harvests with machetes and building roads with nothing but picks and shovels.

Of course, many Ghanaians live well, very well. You see them tooling around Accra's rutted streets in Mercedes-Benzes and BMWs. They live in gated neighborhoods with 24-hour attendants. Yet for the most part, when friends ask, "How was Africa?" I say, "It's not easy."

But then what should one expect in an emerging country struggling with poverty, illiteracy and health problems? In fact, the sooner a visitor accepts Africa on Africa's terms, the sooner he or she can dispense with the bad habits of Westerners, who treat their hosts shabbily and then return home and whine about how poorly they were treated abroad. Anyway, whatever Ghanaians lack in creature comforts-reliable running water, soft toilet paper, fluffy towels-they overly compensate for with extraordinary hospitality.

It helps that, of the 17 nations that constitute modern West Africa, Ghana is essentially an oasis of political stability in a politically unstable region. However, Ghana too has had coups, including one in 1981 that brought current President Jerry Rawlings to power. Rawlings finally was elected after a new constitution adopted in 1992 allowed multiparty contests.

Ghana gained its independence from Britain in 1957. Its first president, Kwame Nkrumah, was an American-educated, Pan Africanist who invited the renowned but beleaguered black scholar W.E.B. DuBois to Africa. DuBois died in Ghana, and today his home in Accra is a museum. There's also a glittering memorial to Nkumah in Accra. However, he was overthrown during the numbing Cold War years when the West was only too glad to help supposed pro-democracy forces get rid of upstart Third World leaders deemed too chummy with Communists.

President Rawlings has political opposition too. His most vociferous watchdogs and critics are in the "private press" championed by Kabral Blay-Amihere and others. I met Kabral in 1990 at Harvard University when we were Nieman Fellows. He is publisher of The Independent newspaper and president of the West Africa Journalists Association.

Frankly, I was impressed by the Ghanaian journalists in the private and government press I met during a tour of the pro-government newspaper, *The Daily Graphic*. Particularly impressive, however, are the journalists who are so dedicated that they work without typewriters and write their stories longhand on strips of newsprint.

Kabral's passion is to develop in West Africa a "serious press," a press, he says, that will not be captive "to the minds of governments, to the whims and caprices of dictators and tyrants." A radical concept indeed in Africa as each day's news brings reports of journalists being arrested for writing what government officials would prefer they not. Ghana, of course, doesn't lack for U.S. and European influences, including private press journalists' ideas about press freedoms.

Ghana's official language is English, and tourism is encouraged. Also countless Ghanaians are studying, traveling and living abroad and have developed tastes for things foreign that they import at home. Don't be surprised if, while sitting in heavy traffic in Accra, which is just about always, you hear American rapper Tupac Shakur on the radio as often as Amakye Dede, a hugely popular Ghanaian entertainer. Meanwhile, Ghana's sole national TV network often features old American westerns, war movies and cartoons with plots wildly out of context in Africa.

Ghana's strategic location, on the Gulf of Guinea, made it a focal point for the notorious slave trade, which, conservatively estimated, saw 15 million Africans forcibly removed from the continent between the 1500s through the mid-1800s. And yes, for those who wish to confer a sort of Good Housekeeping seal of approval on slavery, there were Africans who sold other Africans into slavery.

Outside influences also come from missionaries who've long found Ghana fertile for converts. In the most remote places, one can find advertisements for one church or another. According to one almanac, 62 percent of Ghanaians are Christians, 16 percent are Muslims, and just 21 percent adhere to various traditional beliefs.

The Dutch, Portuguese, French and British all at one time or another exploited Ghana's human and natural resources. And along the way, some Ghanaians have been infused with such disdain for their blackness that they bleach their skin. Many African Americans did the same in the days when our publications were overrun with advertisements for Nadinola and other skin-bleaching products. Ghanaians, apparently, like African Americans, were given the drill: "If you're white, you're right. If you're brown, stick around. But if you're black, get back!"

While three weeks don't make me an expert, I've been rehearsing for my first visit to "The Motherland" ever since shedding the Tarzan complex that used to cause many black Americans to be ashamed of our African roots. It was years before I really appreciated Aunt Catherine's subtlety when she said of me that I was black and beautiful rather than black but beautiful.

History is just that, "his story," and for too long, Africa's was told by her conquerors. Thank goodness, this is no longer the case. Nowadays, Africans tell their own story and mingle with African Americans with the result that we both understand better the commonality of our history.

I was fortunate not to get stuck on the tourist track. I spent most of my three weeks in the company of journalists, ordinary folks, village chiefs and women who touched my soul with their commitment to creating a new reality and future for African women and girls.

I leaned on the walls and gazed out of so-called "doors of no return" at the Elmina and Cape Coast slave castles. In them, I shut my eyes and tried to imagine how awful it must have been when those dank, narrow corridors were filled with people chained together and readied for the journey known as the Middle Passage. It was a tearful and life-changing experience.

I danced in the streets of Tamale during Damba, the annual celebration of Mohammed's birthday, and visited wives in the homes of village chiefs. That Tamale is Louisville's Sister City put me in contact with Razak El-Alawa, editor-in-chief, and other staffers of The New Ghanaian newspaper, a year-old publication dedicated to rousting from their slumber the people of Ghana's three Northern regions, which the editors say have been neglected too long.

Tamale businessman and civic leader Alhaji Aliu Mahama
pressed me to remind African Americans not to limit their
visits to the slave castles of Cape Coast. They should also,
he said, venture north, from where vast numbers of their
ancestors were stolen. Many visitors, for example, have no
knowledge of Babatu, the fierce Niger-born warrior who
captured and sold hundreds of fellow Africans into slavery.
Babatu died in 1909, and his palace and grave are in the
northern Ghanaian city of Yendi.

While in Tamale, I met, broke bread with and danced
joyously with Habiba, Agathar, Mariama, Balchisu, Fati and
Madam Bawa. These women realize that centuries of
subjugation of African women and girls have retarded the
continent's development.

As a result of my trip, I am more offended by Keith R.
Richburg's book, *Out of America*, based on his experiences
of three years of reporting from Africa for *The Washington
Post*. Richburg wrote, "I thank God my nameless ancestor,
brought across the ocean in chains and leg irons, made it out
alive," so that today he's an American and not an African.
Wittingly or not, Richburg's comment has served as proof
positive to certain people that enslaving black people was
somehow beneficial to them.

It is possible, though, to be a proud black American and not
hate Africa and Africans. What's more, it is open to question
how Africa might have developed had she not been invaded
and looted by Europeans. Contrary to popular myth, Daniel
P. Mannix and Malcolm Cowley make clear in their book,
Black Cargoes: A History of the Atlantic Slave Trade, that
Africans were highly developed before the white man came.
"Before Europeans appeared on the coast," they wrote, "the
Negroes of West Africa had created a number of brilliant
empires, one succeeding another. The first to be recorded in
history was Ghana. . . . "The king of Ghana could put
200,000 soldiers into the field. He maintained a system of
highways with rest

houses for travelers at regular intervals. His subjects had fine buildings, a code of laws, and an advanced knowledge of agriculture and medicine." Of course, whatever Africans did not freely share, the foreigners, as they did to Indians in America and other native peoples, took by force and then audaciously called their hosts the savages.

Indeed, the roots of today's ethnic violence in Africa lie in colonialism. Europeans created borders that suited their needs but wreaked havoc on centuries of African life. Richard Trillo and Jim Hudgens, authors of *The Rough Guide to West Africa*, wrote that the West Africa of old was built over many centuries, and that "from this older perspective, the countries of today are imposters, fixed in place by the colonial powers of Britain, France, Germany and Portugal. Although the national borders are established and nationalism is a part of each country's social fabric, the richness and variety of West Africa only comes into focus with some understanding of its ancient past."

A moving experience for me occurred just outside the walls of Elmina slave castle. Children were playing in open drainage areas as sad-eyed women and slack-shouldered men stared blankly at the tourists who regularly invade their space. It was a sorry scene, all the more so as I had read how fierce the inhabitants of the region had been centuries ago in trying to fight off foreign invaders. When I asked Kabral why the children of Elmina don't fall deathly ill playing in such unsanitary conditions, his eyes were as moist as mine. "My Sister," he said, "God takes care of us."

– September 14, 1997

Ghanaian doors fly open

ALL ONE must be is a friend of a friend of a friend-sometimes not even that-for doors to fly open in Ghana. Matter of fact, those unused to such openness may be a bit disconcerted and inclined to mutter a time or two, "Whoa! What do these people really want from me?"

Frankly, the thought did cross my mind the day a woman I had just met on the bus ride from Kumasi to Accra vowed to take me home with her if my ride wasn't at the depot to meet me. Ghanaians did indeed want something from me: that I think well of them individually and that I speak well of their country to people in the United States.

If I sound a bit romantic, indulge me. I am not naive about Africa's problems and complications. Yes, I did meet Ghanaians who seemed infinitely more interested in how I might help them get to America than in me. And yes,

Africa is a continent of recent civil wars and ethnic slaughter, of famine and drought, and of numbing poverty and illiteracy. Truth be told, our media tend to keep us much better informed about Africa's deficiencies than about the new breed of African leaders who are driving out corrupt leaders and are working to form regional economic and military alliances.

Yet for all of Africa's challenges, it isn't unusual to meet foreigners who are smitten with the continent, who went on temporary assignments as missionaries, Peace Corps volunteers or students, for example, and stayed on.

Perhaps they were lured in part by the enveloping peacefulness of nights in remote areas, where the inky darkness is broken only by the light of a full moon, glittering stars, the occasional passing car or the glow from the candles of vendors illuminating their kiosks.

My hosts in Ghana's northern region were the Tamale Municipal Assembly and members of the Tamale-Louisville Sister City Committee. Daniel Nyankamawu, the point man, arranged for Dr. Tracy K'Meyer, a University of Louisville history professor with whom I flew to Ghana, and me to stay in a guest house.

Our accommodations were clean and sparse. The big thing about Spartan living-no telephone, no television and no radio-is how it evoked in me a heightened sense of spiritual connectedness. I spent my late nights in Tamale, for example, reading *Miles*, the 1989 autobiography by the late jazz trumpeter Miles Davis in collaboration with Quincy Troupe. In that setting, I found myself doing a lot more than reading. I was experiencing Miles Davis, much in the way I experience his music at home.

I do not doubt that all who go to Africa are changed in some way by the sweeping contradictions of nature and man; the grinding poverty side by side with breathtaking natural beauty. While in Ghana I found beauty in the most ordinary things: the face of a little village girl who kept peeking around her mother and smiling at me so that I just had to pick her up, and the laughter of uniformed school boys in Tema playing soccer during recess and not minding a request to have their picture taken with a visitor. And I was blown away at how, in the midst of teeming Accra, rows of Muslim men would stop, lay down their mats, fall to their knees and press their heads to the ground while being led in prayer by unseen imams whose voices filtered through loudspeakers outside overcrowded mosques.

For an African American, going to Africa can be especially poignant. It is strange for us to be some place where, for once, we aren't a minority-where all authority resides with people who look like us.

The TV anchors are black; the experts are black; and for the most part, the lawyers, doctors, teachers, corporate executives, entrepreneurs, longshoremen and museum curators are black too. One needn't yearn for role models in Africa.

Tracy K'Meyer mentioned several times having a similar experience, but in reverse-of being white and in the minority. Personally, it felt good simply not to stand out-to feel, everywhere and at every moment, absolutely at ease in my own skin.

I often write about how God works in my life, and my first visit to Africa is a case in point. It was providence that on the same day that a friend reneged on our plans for a Caribbean cruise, Dr. Susan Broadhead Herlin of the University of Louisville invited me to visit Ghana. It wasn't a fluke, either, that one of the dearest associations cultivated during my Nieman Fellowship year was between myself and Kabral Blay-Amihere and his family.

After six years, Kabral and I were reunited in Ghana. His connections opened doors for me and put me in touch with Ghanaian journalists.

Of course, it isn't dumb luck that Tamale and Louisville are Sister Cities in a relationship going back to 1979. Or that two women I knew, Susan Broadhead Herlin and Erma Bush, are co-chairwomen of the Louisville-Tamale committee. In inviting me to Ghana to meet with, encourage and forge a long-term relationship with the staff of The New Ghanaian, Susan was performing one of her duties as Tamale's Zo-Simli-Naa, which means chief of friendship, love and peace. (Sister Cities, by the way, is a volunteer organization that seeks to cultivate international partnerships.). I'd say that the stars were all lined up in just the right order for me finally to get to Africa.

And to me, how this trip came about, starting with a friend backing out of a commitment, proves yet again that my dear mother was right when she used to say, "Betty, when one door closes, God will open another one." God did, and I thank Him.   – September 18, 1997

Peeking into Cuba today

I DIDN'T know quite what to expect as the decrepit Russian-made airliner sputtered toward Cuba from the Bahamas. When my mind wasn't focused on my fear of flying in that ancient bucket, I was reflecting on the fact that I was on my way to Fidel Castro's island, which for 40 years has been off-limits to all but a few Americans.

But here I was, on my way to Havana with eight other members of the William Monroe Trotter Group, a collective of African-American columnists.

What a time to be making the trip! Fidel Castro and most Cubans on the island are apoplectic over 6-year-old Elián Gonzalez. At the time, the child, who was plucked from the ocean by fishermen in November, was still in Miami with distant relatives, despite his father's repeated pleas that the boy be returned to him in Cardenas, Cuba.

Elián's mother, Elizabet, and 13 others died at sea attempting to reach the U. S. illegally. (Many Americans may not be aware that the U. S. and Cuba do have an agreement that allows some 20,000 Cubans legally to emigrate here each year.)

President Clinton, the U. S. Immigration and Naturalization Service, Attorney General Janet Reno and a majority of Americans and Cubans are on the same page relative to Elián.

page 77

But fiercely anti-Castro Cubans in Miami feel otherwise, and they've proven to be stubborn and politically astute. So Elián remains here, where Miami Cubans say he'll have a better life and more opportunities.

But, as I would soon learn, Cubans are chagrined. They seem amazed that their Miami cousins have so much influence over the U.S. legal system. In fact, they often referred to Cuban-American exile leaders as "Mafia," spitting the word when they say it.

I've traveled to many countries, but of all airplanes that have borne me, the Cubana Airlines jet was the oldest. This was my first experience in a plane with no doors on the overhead luggage racks. We stuffed our carry-on bags up there and then prayed nothing would fly off and hit us on the head.

Flight attendants came through with their carts. The rum and ham sandwiches were free, but fruit juice cost a dollar. Passengers also could buy perfume, Cuban cigars and cigarettes from the cart.

Despite stabs at small talk with my seatmate, Sheryl McCarthy of *Newsday*, I was quiet and nervous during the flight. *USA Today* columnist DeWayne Wickham, who organized the trip (partially underwritten by the Freedom Forum) sat across the aisle with Norman Lockman, of *The News Journal* in Wilmington, Del. In typical dude fashion, they were cool.

Since I don't indulge in alcohol, I had nothing to quell my jitters other than DeWayne's comforting observation: "You've got to figure that people who can keep their cars running for 40 years must be able to do the same thing for their airplanes." When we landed without incident at José Martí Airport, named for the 19th-century poet and revolutionary, the passengers gave the Cuban pilot and his crew heartfelt applause.

Some in our group were shocked when they picked up a free Cuban newspaper at the airport and found editorial cartoons depicting Haitians in most unflattering way-with oversized lips, breasts and behinds. I passed on opportunities to buy Cuban dolls and other tourist items that carried the negative depictions.

But Cubans, by and large, as we discovered, apparently don't have the same hang-ups on matters of race as do Americans. Several Afro-Cubans insisted that race isn't a serious issue in Cuba since "the triumph of the Revolution," as they called it.

Rather than being ugly and demeaning, the black Cubans said they considered the imagery beautiful.

Cuba has a little more than 11 million people. Most receive free health care, and all schools are free and run by the government. A substantial number of Cubans pay no rent or taxes, and one in every 10 reportedly has guaranteed social security. Over 1 million are receiving pensions.

"Education and public health are still prioritized sectors, accounting for 39 percent" of Cuba's national budget, according to information provided by the Cuban Interest Section in Washington, D. C.

Tourism has become an important source of the precious dollars necessary to finance Castro's Socialist dreams. The section reported 1.4 million tourists in 1998, mostly from Canada, Italy, Spain, Germany, France, England, Mexico, Argentina, Colombia and Portugal. The country's gross receipts from tourism that year totaled some $900 million.

Cuba has about 30,000 hotel rooms, and plans to add 4,000 by year's end. Government officials say they expect 2 million visitors in 2000.

Some of Cuba's hotels are completely government-owned, but most of the newer ones are joint ventures with foreign investors. It's mandatory, we were told, that Cubans share management responsibilities.

Most of what we Americans read and hear about Cuba and its leader, Fidel Castro, isn't exactly positive. And mostly, how we feel about Cuba, sight unseen, is bent through the prism of the Cold War, which may be over everywhere else but not between the U. S. and Cuba. Still, every now and then, Americans can read warm tales of successful U.S.-Cuban cultural exchanges, and President Clinton has made moves in the direction of easing relations.

But something always seems to happen, like the Elián González case, or the recent arrest of a Cuban-born INS official who is accused of being a spy.

Quite frankly, I expected to be overwhelmed by Castro's persona. But it's not Castro's image that shows up most often on buildings and billboards. It's Che Guevara's.

The 40-year economic blockade of Cuba by the U. S. obviously has badly wounded the island's economy. Cuba claims that U.S. interventions have cost it $65 billion over the years.

Increasingly, however, more Americans believe the embargo is counterproductive – but for different reasons. It not only stirs anti-U.S. feelings, some say, but it also gives Castro cover for his failed Socialist experiment.

Whatever the case, Cuba is a poor country. But it's hardly the poorest, and is far from being the worst-off among developing nations. In fact, Cuba's health and education statistics are better than those of its non-Communist Caribbean and Latin American neighbors. In many vital statistics, Cuba matches or surpasses most industrialized nations, including the U.S. But more about that later.

Heading into Havana, which is on Cuba's northern coast, one observes palm-tree-lined streets reminiscent of Southern California. Other sections look very much like some European capitals.

Overall, I imagined preservationists getting heartburn over the neglect that claims so many of Havana's historic buildings. There's so much disrepair; many buildings are simply crumbling.

Supreme Court President Ruben Remigio Ferro was almost apologetic that his court is now situated in such modest quarters. He said that the court's real home, a beautiful old building, has badly deteriorated, and there's not enough money to restore it.

Countless structures in Havana with incredible architectural value scream out for paint and high-velocity hose-downs.

Our hotel, the Parque Central in Old Havana, isn't among them. A joint Cuban government/Swiss venture, the hotel is very European in look and service. It faces a bustling thoroughfare and Central Park, where in the evenings Cubans gather to laugh, talk, flirt or soak up the street sounds, including pulsating Latin rhythms coming from somewhere off in the distance.

On our first evening in Havana, Norm Lockman and I
strolled around the park. We also ventured off the main
drag, and found darkness, broken unevenly by flickering TV
sets and naked light bulbs inside the open doors of
apartments.

What if someone pounced?

But the Cubans paid us no mind. Anyway, they would be
hard-pressed to identify us as tourists since a large
proportion of Cubans-we asked how many, but got many
different numbers, one as high as 65 percent and another as
low as 20 percent-share with us a common ancestry; they're
also black.

And I read a tourist advisory that said hassling tourists in
Cuba is a serious no-no. A prostitute can get five years in
jail, a pimp 20 years, and a Cuban could be sentenced to up
to 70 years for attacking a tourist.

Norm and I ventured deeper into the darkness, following
the sounds of music. We stopped at a rundown, graffiti-
covered building; just as we arrived, the door opened, to let
someone out, and a smiling Cuban invited us in.

We couldn't believe what was going on behind that door. It
was a nightclub. The band was jamming, and people were
dancing up a storm. Having grown up a Latin music lover in
East Harlem, I was in heaven. In minutes, Norm and I were
on the floor dancing.

There were no classes in Cuban schools the week of our
visit. Our tour guide, Orlando, said that since many parents
work, school holidays are used for organized field trips. We
saw school busloads of Cuban children. Many were visiting
museums; others were frolicking in parks.

Cuba, which would fit 83 times into the U.S., has 200
museums, 121 art galleries, 50 theaters, 326 bookshops,
350 libraries, 56 schools of art, and a national ballet
company, according to the Cuban Interest Section in
Washington, D. C.

I'm hardly an expert after only a week, but my eyes and
heart told me that the best thing that happened to Cuba was
the collapse of the Soviet Union, the country's former main
benefactor.

The Soviets introduced into that lovely country the most hideous-looking automobiles, as well as sinfully ugly, cement-block housing that seems so out of place in the lush countryside.

The Soviet collapse 10 years ago forced Cuba's Communist leaders to restructure the economy. Certain things are rationed, we heard, especially milk and eggs. But now, U.S. dollars and more foreign investments are welcome. Americans, however, must walk around with lots of cash, because the U.S. embargo prohibits transactions that involve U.S. banks.

"Did you feel as if you were being watched?" I've been asked.

Actually, I didn't. But I'd be lying if I said there wasn't an obvious police presence around our hotel and others nearby. Hotel security men, with wires hanging out of their ears, were a constant presence in the lobby. Cubans apparently aren't allowed to visit tourists in their rooms.

This could be construed as official repression, but the explanation is that the limits are set to minimize opportunities for crime, such as drug dealing and prostitution.

I heard that ordinary Cubans are afraid to talk to tourists on the streets. I didn't find that to be true. Many Cubans wanted to talk, growing excited when they discovered we were Americans. Inevitably, they'd ask about Elián and say that he should come home. But three young Cubans, who appeared to be in their late teens or early 20s, weren't so sure. "It's too poor here," they said in a conversation outside the Museum of the Revolution.

Two Afro-Cubans I chatted with said they used to live in the U. S., but had been deported. I dared not ask why. One, who said he lived in Harlem in the 1940s, was overcome. "I'm an Afro," he said several times beating on his chest, "just like you!" The other Cuban, who was in his 30s and was walking with his wife and daughter, was puffing on a fat cigar. He said he'd gone to school in Yonkers, N. Y. His mother is still there, and he's been trying without success to get back.

And yes, Havana's streets resemble nothing so much as a giant antique car showroom. There are, however, a surprising number of newer cars, but many of them, I noticed, had tourism tags. Most ordinary Cubans get around on foot, bicycles or buses, including weird-looking double-decker models.

My most unexpected sight in Cuba was a huge bust of Abraham Lincoln in a park in the middle of Havana that honors the 16th president along with other "heroes of the Americas." But on second thought, it makes sense that Lincoln would be there because Africans were enslaved in Cuba too.

– February 27, 2000

Discrimination outlawed in Cuba, but attitudes persist

CUBANS WERE proud to tell visiting African Americans there is no racial discrimination there. It's against the law in Cuba. It's a perversion of the ideal that all Cubans-black, white and mestizo (mixed race), are equal in Fidel Castro's Cuba. Nonetheless, issues of race and discrimination provoked some of the liveliest discussions members of the William Trotter Group had with Cubans.

"Negritos take part in everything just like whites," said Ruben Remigio Ferro, the first black of the 19 Supreme Court presidents since 1899. "The vast majority of judges and non-professional judges are blacks or mestizos,"

he said. And "three years ago, the majority in jail were not black or mestizo, and we were surprised. Forty percent were black and mestizos, and 60 percent were white."

Those statistics raised eyebrows within our delegation, as they defy conventional wisdom (ours) that crime follows poverty. Everything we had heard and read told us that the poorest Cubans are mostly black.

Nonetheless, the chief justice, who was only a child when Castro rose to power 41 years ago, insisted.

He edged forward in his chair and said with great passion: "Before the revolution, discrimination was a reality we faced. Before the revolution, there were never any black people on the Supreme Court. Before the revolution, you needed to have money to study law." His own career, Ferro noted, is a "triumph" of the revolution.

Page 84

"I come from a humble family. My father was a farmer and my mother was a housewife. We are eight brothers."
American travel writer and Latin American scholar Mark Cramer is the author of *Culture Shock! Cuba.* In it, he writes that no matter what one's feelings may be about Castro, "since the early '60s, Cuba has been experimenting, sometimes groping, for ways to create a society in which social equality is the norm."
Today, Afro-Cubans are represented well in the highest professions, and since 1997, after some grumbling, more are members of the Cuban Communist Party's central committee. Indeed, according to Cramer, "There is still greater equality among Cubans than one finds within any other Latin American country."
Our probings about race may explain the impatience of an Afro-Cuban journalist in the press delegation we met with at the Jose Marti International Institute of Journalism. "You make us think about things that we don't think about," he said.
We asked why, for example, despite Cuba's majority black and mestizo population, most of the workers at our hotel were white Cubans. The question's relevance is that tourism workers have access to dollars, now that the government, as an economic stimulus, has legalized their use.
Cubans with dollars can buy food, material goods and even some medicines that Cubans with pesos cannot.
Later, leaders of one of Cuba's religious groups, the Yoruba Association, echoed what others had said-that Cuba is a non-discriminatory society. The Yoruba faith has roots in West Africa, and is widely practiced today in former slave colonies such as Cuba and Haiti, and in the U.S. in many heavily Caribbean communities.
We asked the Yorubas about "remittances," money that Cubans abroad send back to relatives. Since most Cubans abroad are white, the majority of remittances, we deduced, are being sent to white Cubans, which puts Afro-Cubans at a distinct economic disadvantage. But Castenada, head of the Yoruba Association, rejected the premise and the definition

of "white." "We don't feel that we have problems (relative to race), but when they (Cubans) get to the U. S., they lose their Cuban accents and say that they are white." Those "white" Cubans, Castenada insisted, do, in fact, send remittances back to black relatives, he said.

Our tour guide, Orlando, a white Cuban, said the revolution's great achievement is that it brought unity among the races. Still, Orlando said that there are Cubans and foreign investors in the country whose "attitudes" result in "certain ways of discrimination."

In November, at a Trotter conference in Atlanta, Felix Hernandez, the Afro-Cuban head of the Cuban Interest Section in Washington, said some Cubans do prefer that their children select white or light-skinned mates.

African Americans describe such people as "color-struck."

Those attitudes, according to one of our country's leading Afrocentric scholars, Na'im Akbar, grow out of notions of white supremacy, "the philosophical thought that there is a natural superiority of white over black." What's more, those attitudes defy political ideology, he said, which explains why they exist even in Cuba. Some say that one way Cuba's tourist industry gets around the official ban on discrimination is to assess the "appearance" of black Cubans, even if they're highly qualified, as being unacceptable to visitors from abroad.

Still, Cubans agree that though there are similarities between experiences of African Americans and Afro-Cubans, Cuba has never had such policies as segregated transportation or separate public bathrooms and water fountains.

But given Cuba's history of "certain attitudes," many argue that Castro's power depends heavily on Afro-Cubans, who presumably have most benefited from the revolution. Maybe so. But Cuba scholar Alejandro de la Fuente believes that view is based on an "unverified" assumption that "white Cubans desire change more than blacks."

In a paper, "Recreating Racism: Race and Discrimination in Cuba's 'Special Period'," de la Fuente acknowledges that Castro "did open significant opportunities for all sectors of the population regardless of race." And a 1994 survey, he noted, found that 94 percent of Cubans believed that "skin color does not significantly affect opportunities."

But Cuba's so-called "Special Period," de la Fuente said, is taking a toll. It has "severely limited the state's capacity to distribute goods and services to the population." The government's economic stimuli, such as legalizing use of U. S. dollars and chasing foreign investments and tourists, have "provoked increasing inequality and resentment in the population used to living in a highly egalitarian setting."

Indeed, we African-American guests in Cuba deeply respected the views of Cubans, even when deep down we may have considered them naive and romantic.

But we also wondered how long they will be content living with economic disparities similar to those that existed before Fidel. Time will tell.

— March 2, 2000

Chapter Six:

Interiors

Living through the 'power surges'

IT PAINS ME to think that I actually accused my mother of faking when, in her 40s, she'd do get depressed or cry for no apparent reason.

"Don't worry, your day will come," she'd say when I responded to her by saying: "Mommy. Not again!" And then there were the times my mother's sisters would visit. It was like a ritual. They'd sit around our kitchen and living room sweating, fanning and throwing open windows in the wintertime.

"Don't worry, your day will come," one aunt inevitably would say when I'd make fun of them.

Well, my day has come. I'm saying it aloud. I'm one of the millions of baby-boomer women who, as one writer put it, finds herself "crossing the hormonal divide, kicking and screaming as usual for information and attention."

More explicitly, I'm "changing life."

I'm experiencing what Gail Sheehy, in the title of her bestseller, refers to as *The Silent Passage: Menopause.*

Overlook the small m in menopause. Millions of women, I'm sure, will testify that what Sheehy calls "a normal physical process" is actually no small thing at all.

Naturally, there's a medical definition for menopause. But I'm no doctor; I'm just a woman going through it. So, in laywoman's terms, I describe menopause as the time when a woman's childbearing years are ending and all the stuff nature equipped us with to make childbearing possible, like

page 88

estrogen and progesterone, no longer have much to do.

Fortunately, my mother and aunts haven't demanded my apology for making light of what was occurring when they were going through "The Change." I suppose my mother and aunts understood then the arrogance of youth.

In fact, I've been "changing life" for a couple of years. I'm not ashamed to say that I'm experiencing such things as an irregular menstrual cycle, memory lapses and flourishes of irritability that occasionally even catch me unaware.

And with increasing regularity, I'm having to endure the often-joked about "hot flashes." In fact, hot flashes are anything but funny, especially if they occur when you're unable to rip off your clothes, snatch off your wig, or delve into your briefcase for anything suitable with which to fan.

Despite all that, it's only been recently that my body has gotten my full attention. I'm coming to understand that if I don't take care of me, I certainly can't be there for others. So these days, I'm listening to what my body is saying. I'm trying to educate myself now that I'm aware that there's

a lot more to menopause than what most of us have learned from those old wives' tales about the changes that "The Change" is likely to bring.

Besides a trip to the gynecologist and reading Sheehy's book, I recently attended a gathering of women with the not-very-discreet title: "Taking Control of Mid-Life: The Silent Passage Conference."

About 700 women braved snow and ice hear Sheehy and to learn what was happening to us from experts who led discussions on such topics as "To Hysterectomy or not to Hysterectomy? That is the Question" and "What You're Looking for is not in Your Purse."

Laughter rippled through the audience as Sheehy threw out one-liners like: "Women don't have hot flashes. They have power surges." And it was heartening to hear Sheehy say that, unlike in our mothers' and grandmothers' time, menopausal women in the 1990s aren't suffering in silence. We're "coming out" so to speak. We're demanding more of our doctors, and we're talking among ourselves, even forming fan-and-hot-flashes clubs.

One of the myths about menopause is that a woman in her 30s or early 40s is too young to be going through it. In fact, Dr. Christine Cook, an associate professor at the University of Louisville School of Medicine, told women at the conference that fertility actually begins to decline as early as 25 until about age 37. After that, she said, the decline becomes more rapid.

I've also discovered that while virtually all women will experience menopause, often with similar symptoms, none of us is likely to do it in precisely the same way. "The change of life is idosyncratic," Sheehy says.

"It's like a thumbprint: Everybody is different."

Often a little education can be dangerous, but that no education can kill you. That's why I want to shout from the rooftops and let women in my age group everywhere know that they must hold on, and that if they take care of themselves, it's really going to be all right.

There is life after menopause, the experts say.

Indeed, Sheehy says many women argue that it's an even better life; a life unfettered by fears of intimacy leading to pregnancy. It's often the case that women in their 50s and 60s feel that they've finally got license to say exactly what's on their minds. That's because, according to Sheehy, it's during those years that all the lessons a woman has learned come together.

It's then that our feminine and masculine qualities learn to co-exist, making it possible, Sheehy says, for us to claim our place as "one of the culture's wise women."

And what, I ask, can be better than being a woman and wise to boot?

– March 18, 1993

Keeping promises

IT'S EVERY public speaker's nightmare to be handed a topic about which he or she knows little or lacks enthusiasm. Kind audiences sit stoically through boring speeches and dutifully deliver polite applause at the end.

Hundreds of hours over a lifetime of ingesting speeches leaves no doubt that there are some that may knock 'em dead in Brooklyn but won't cut the mustard in Peoria.

Speechmaking is not for the fainthearted. From experience, I can attest that lurking beneath seemingly cool, calm, collected exteriors of many public speakers are stomachs that churn nonstop until the amen is said and the waiters have begun to clear the tables.

Getting up before a crowd is more difficult than imagined by many friends, who say: "We don't care what you talk about. We know it'll be good."

Now that's faith. Unfortunately, faith doesn't diminish the reality that delivering a speech to strangers is to expose oneself to as much potential ridicule as potential praise.

What speaker, for example, can predict a coughing spell in the middle of the text? An inexplicable stutter over every word that begins with the letter "t"?

Or the loud, persistent boor-there's always one-who feels compelled to compete for the audience's attention?

And how about those occasional zinger questions from the audience that leave a speaker physically standing on her feet but intellectually down for the count?

Unlike a bad singer, a public speaker doesn't have a backup group to scream louder when the featured performer is clearly going down the tubes. Public speaking is more akin to being a standup comic-when you get out in front of the crowd, you're on your own.

Such thoughts percolated when I contemplated preparing a recent speech. The days before a big speech are invariably the same.

There's nervousness. And nagging questions: What if I trip and fall walking across the stage? What if no one laughs at my supposedly sidesplitting lines? What if I spy eyes that say, "I'm trying to hang in there with you, sister, but I fail to get your point."

Mercifully, this particular invitation to speak came with a theme: "Promises to Keep." I loved it immediately.

"Promises to Keep." Now that's rich. That's a subject ripe to be explored for 20 minutes or so with an audience of women. Mentally, I played the theme over and over, and I realized how my life and the lives of many women I know actually revolve around promises kept and unkept.

Many women wait hours by the phone for promised calls that never come; calls for a date, a part in a movie, or a job.

And how about the battered sisters who, after a fifth black eye, third broken arm or second broken leg, say pitifully, "He promised he wouldn't beat me or the kids the next time he and the world had a disagreement."

"Promises to Keep" reminds me of a mother who, way back in the 1950s, when such things were rarely done, failed to keep her promises to two young daughters, abandoning them to an essentially motherless fate. That mother, as pretty as a sunny day in May, left the girls to pursue a life of being wined and dined by handsome men who loved pretty women like her but didn't want to be bothered with her "brats."

Today, that mother sits in a nursing home. Beauty has fled, and she can barely remember what happened yesterday, much less her broken promise of 40 years ago.

Daughters forgive, of course, but they never forget.

"Promises to Keep" is a theme to be explored with women, many of whom cling to promises that life should have taught them by now cannot and won't ever be kept.

"Promises to Keep" reminds me that were it not for promises, some women's lives would be unbearable. It's a reminder that the line between promises and dreams blur, and that promises and dreams often are one and the same.

Meanwhile, if there's any point I hope I was able to make with the women who heard me this week, it's this: As important as it is for women to keep our promises to others, it's just as important that we learn to keep our promises to ourselves.

– March 30, 1995

Breathing easy

ON JUNE 12, 1990, I found myself sitting among 100 or so strangers in a hotel ballroom. Practically none of us were there because we wished to be.

Most of us, questioning revealed, had been either gently coaxed or scared into coming.

I got scared after seeing Sammy Davis Jr. on television a few weeks earlier. The "Candy Man" was dying.

Sammy Davis and my dad had a few things in common. They were about the same height. Had about the same skin coloring. Were about the same in stature. And both were blind in one eye.

I, in Louisville, and my mother, in New York City, just happened to be watching the television tribute to Sammy. It must have been mental telepathy, but my mother called and said, "Doesn't Sammy remind you of how your father looked before he died?"

Sammy Davis and Daddy both were hooked on nicotine. Ultimately, it was nicotine that helped kill them.

When famous people die, they demand our attention. So Sammy Davis' death gave me yet another incentive to do what I had been contemplating for years.

Still I went to the stop-smoking seminar only half-believing the hype. It wasn't easy to sell me on the notion that for just $35, I could forever kick my habit. Cigarettes had claimed a part of my every waking hour for 28 years.

Thus, when I finally decided two years ago to try hypnosis to stop smoking, I didn't tell my friends, fearing I'd have to hear the "I told you so" refrains if I failed. And I certainly was in no mood for smug sermonettes from people who had never been hooked: "Girl, all you need is will power."

No. What I needed was help.

Help because I still wasn't absolutely convinced that smoking was all that bad. In fact, I rather enjoyed the practice. Cigarettes had always given me confidence in strange or uncomfortable situations. Years ago, I believed a cigarette dangling between my fingers made me appear more sophisticated, made me not look out of place in bars and nightclubs.

I also believed cigarettes aided me in writing. My ashtray was always full of butts. Occasionally, I'd forget and have two cigarettes going at once.

Plus, I'd seen many cool photographs of my writer-idols looking beautiful, intellectual and poignant, peering out from behind the wispy curls of smoke from their cigarettes.

Anyone who died from a smoking-related ailment, I figured, obviously had weak genes. Millions of longtime smokers live to get old without any apparent problems.

Of course, I often comforted myself with the smoker's creed: "We're all going to die of something."

Well, I've watched loved ones who loved to smoke die. And it wasn't pretty.

I'll always remember Uncle Artie, stricken with emphysema, slowly making his way around his last family reunion toting a portable oxygen machine. Uncle Artie had the same defeated look I had seen in my father, who had died a month earlier.

Cancer of the lung and throat didn't stop my father from smoking. He said it didn't make sense to stop since he already had cancer.

Did that stop me from smoking? No!

I also recall when my father, a gregarious sort, stopped being able to talk. I remember how he looked longingly at the solid foods he no longer could eat.

Did that stop me from smoking? No!

Oh, how my father loved those strong, unfiltered cigarettes in the red pack. My mother still does. Daddy's love affair cost him his life at 59. Mommy was a widow at 55.

But did I stop smoking? No!

Still, I pledged that if I ever did quit, I'd not be like many reformed addicts. I'd not meddle and harass friends who couldn't or didn't wish to kick the habit. So, I don't nag my smoker friends. I'm sympathetic to their addiction.

However, if my smoking friends were to ask what motivated me to quit, I'd tell them that I'm glad to be liberated from the desire to grab a couple of puffs every few minutes.

I might even say that I now know that smoking isn't particularly cute. It really does stink. Stinks up your hair. Stinks up your clothes. Stinks up your home. Discolors your teeth. Sours your breath. But if you're a smoker, you hardly notice, and people usually don't mention it.

If a friend who still smokes asks, I'd tell her how I've saved about $4,750 in just two years. They'd be surprised to discover that the money they spend on cigarettes might be enough to pay tuition at some colleges, build a pretty nice wardrobe, or cover the cost of a very, very nice Caribbean cruise.

I'd be lying if I said I don't miss smoking from time to time. And I'm eventually going to die of something. Yet I hope my decision to battle and overcome my nicotine addiction will give me a few more years to enjoy.

But unless they ask, my smoking friends will get no lecture from me. Some don't need lecturing. They know the facts, but they still don't want to quit-even though I wish they would.

Meanwhile, I'm going to celebrate my second anniversary, as a non-smoker.

Thanks, Dad. Thank you too, Sammy.

– June 11, 1992

Discovering your personal power

"That's it!" I told myself after a half-hour in the express line at my supermarket.

A young cashier having a problem with an elderly patron needed help. Three times he summoned a manager over the loudspeaker. Minutes passed. Help never came. And my rage surged.

The store's regulars, of course, weren't surprised that the impasse ultimately resolved itself when the frustrated customer returned the groceries and moved out of line.

By the time I rolled my shopping cart out into the sunshine, I knew that the decision I'd been toying with for months finally had been made. The large supermarket chain probably won't miss the $100 or so I spent each week at its West Louisville store. Such a pittance probably isn't significant to an operation that rakes in millions annually from its stores in neighborhoods with demographics similar to mine.

Still I'm just as fed up with second-class treatment simply because of my zip code and simply because many of my neighbors lack the incomes or transportation that would allow them to buy the competition and respect others take for granted when they're shopping.

I'm fed up with inflated prices-a penny here, a dime there-for staples on welfare- and Social Security-check days.

And goodness knows I've seen too much at-ti-tude from many employed in stores where I live. Why, I'm even old enough to remember when the motto of most stores was "Service with a smile."

As far as I know, my money and my neighbor's money is as green as the money spent by people who live and shop in economically upscale zones.

On many occasions I haven't been able to resist butting in when I've seen fellow shoppers being treated shabbily by store clerks and paying for the privilege!

Of course, mistreatment of any sort causes me grief. But I'm especially enraged when I come across African Americans mistreating other African Americans simply because they can; simply because some of us apparently

believe, as do others, that black people aren't entitled to respectful treatment.

When I've seen shabby treatment, an all-too-frequent occurence in the supermarket I'll no longer patronize, I'm hurt because I know that many meting out the mistreatment seem to have forgotten. They've forgotten that they likely wouldn't have those jobs if somebody-perhaps one of the people forced to wait in a checkout line too long- had not protested to local merchants, saying, "You'll not find business success here unless you hire at least some people from the neighborhood."

So my decision to stop, in effect, endorsing my own mistreatment at my local supermarket is late in coming. Late because for years, personal protests have been an integral part of my repertoire for living.

I boycott people and businesses when I'm made aware that they've made comments or taken actions intended to do me physical, spiritual or psychological harm.

I've boycotted artists who performed in South Africa even though they were politely begged not to do so to help speed the death of apartheid. Once conscious of the mistreatment of migrant workers, I did as the late Cesar Chavez asked and didn't buy California grapes.

I realize that an individual who decides not to spend $16.98 for a compact disc, $25 to attend a concert, or $7 to see a first-run movie isn't likely to stop the show. But history informs that individuals usually have more power than they realize and more power than the powers-that-be want them to know they have.

Of course, when individual power translates into collective power, things change.

Take Montgomery, Ala., where way back in 1955, black people boycotted city buses for nearly a year. They were protesting having to pay full fare and then being forced either to sit in the back of the buses or to stand if a white person paying the identical fare demanded their seat.

But whether it's in Montgomery in 1955, or West Louisville in 1993, mass protests always have their roots in individuals who decided that enough is enough; who decide, as the late civil rights activist Fannie Lou Hamer did, that they're sick and tired of being sick and tired.

Personal protests are great for the spirit. Better yet, they are great examples for people who believe they are absolutely powerless against the Goliaths in our world today. Deciding not to patronize my local supermarket and not to support some artists, athletes, politicians, religious leaders and others who don't have my best interests at heart is small testimony to the power of the individual, even if it's nothing more than deciding where to spend my hard-earned money.

And individual power in our capitalistic system is all the more potent because the urge to make money, and lots of it, usually will supercede any stupid desire to discriminate.

There's solace in knowing that I live in a world where, over centuries, many individuals have discovered their power and have used it to effect positive change.

– September 9, 1993

Finding out what's it all about

You pull the cover over your head. You try to blot out the sun and the loud chirping of birds perched outside your window.

You try hard to squeeze out just a few more minutes, seconds even, before the jarring wail of the alarm clock.

You're a busy person, a concerned, committed and caring individual. The evidence is the plaques and certificates that line your walls.

You're blessed with a modicum of personal and professional success.

But you pay the price.

You're in a perpetual state of tiredness. If you're honest, you may admit that you're also in a perpetual state of low-frequency rage because you're mortal and weren't built to do it all.

But you try.

The result is that sometimes you forget to be kind to the people closest to you. You believe they understand and they love you in spite of your occasional outbursts.

Usually they do understand. But sometimes they don't, even though they know you'd walk through fire and slay a dragon for them if the need arose.

But it's been weeks, months, in some cases years since you've taken quality time for yourself. Quality time to read a book unrelated to your job.

Quality time to pamper and spoil your mate or your kids.

It's always work, work, work. Because it pays the bills, work comes first.

You're a busy man. You're a successful woman. People look up to you. And that compels you to run faster and faster. It's not a part of your nature to disappoint others.

When you're a busy person, even sleep conspires against you. It only gets good when it's almost time to get up. And often, even when you're supposed to be asleep, you're not.

Your eyes are closed. You're lying down. The problem is your mind. It doesn't cooperate. It doesn't fall off to sleep until it's good and ready.

So behind closed eyes, your mind is busily contemplating what's ahead: the meetings, the mail, the speeches, the out-of-town seminars and conferences.

But suddenly, the alarm is wailing insistently. Get up! Get up! Time to get moving!

There's a conspiracy against those of us who never learn to say no. I'm talking to all the busy men and busy women. I'm talking to myself, my colleagues and my friends. We frequently say we ought to get together socially, but we don't because we're too busy.

What's the line that prompts you to cram one engagement too many onto your calendar?

"They need you" is the one that usually makes me overcommit.

Ultimately, it boils down to the question from the classic song, "Alfie."

"What's it all about?"

In the end, who really cares if you wear yourself to a frazzle trying to live up to others' expectations?

In the end, some who used to say they loved you may comment behind your back: "Gee, he looks bad." Or "My, my, she is getting fat."

What's it all about?

Trying to meet others' demands until there's nothing left to give?

What's it all about?

Exhausting yourself to the point that people who once said they needed you, now say, "Let's get someone else"?

When there's no you left, no one needs you.

On Saturday, my phone rang. It was Pat informing me that her brother-in-law, my childhood friend George Richardson, had died.

The news is sobering. I appreciate anew and feel somewhat depressed that, in addition to my parents' and grandparents' friends, my friends also are dying of natural causes.

I mourn my fallen comrade, the smiling boy who used to live one floor up, and I wonder: "What's it all about?"

Whoever first said life's too short knew what she or he was talking about.

It's nice to be successful, to be looked up to, to be really needed. But life's too short to be too busy not to deliberately carve out time to observe and smell the flowers.

In the midst of thinking about George's life, the fun we had when we were kids and his dying at just 51, the phone rang again.

"Wanna go to Hawaii?"

With no hesitation, I scream: "Yes!"

I race to the credit union to make a withdrawal to put a down payment on the trip. In no time, the check's in the mail.

Hawaii! How sweet it is. But alas, the trip isn't until July. What to do in the meantime?

Maybe I should try to get some sleep.

– March 16, 1995

A steamy saga but to what end?

PASSAGES from Georgia Davis Powers' autobiography, I Shared the Dream: The Pride, Passion and Politics of the First Black Woman Senator from Kentucky, read like a steamy pulp novel.

"Days passed uneventfully. Nights quietly. Then, one morning I awoke startled from a dream I'd been having. Dr. Martin Luther King Jr. and I had been together in a hotel room. He was nude, and we were about to make love.

I was frightened, as I had no conscious sensual attraction towards him."

Later, however, Powers claims the dream became reality.

Once, when they were together in Chicago, she asked Dr. King if he believed God predestined her to be with him that night.

"'Definitely,'" she writes he replied. "'You are destined to be here right now with me,' and smiled, looking into my eyes. Later he slept quietly and peacefully as I held him."

This is the stuff of which bestsellers, or hoped-for bestsellers, are made.

The autobiography's title is a play on Dr. King's famous "I Have a Dream" speech. The book's cover features former state Sen. Powers and Dr. King; he's in the foreground, she's in the background.

In publishing, such decisions aren't happenstance. The clear intention is to pump up the volume on Powers' relationship with Dr. King.

page 103

The late Ralph Abernathy, Dr. King's close friend, wrote in his autobiography that a woman he identified only as a member of the Kentucky legislature was with Dr. King the night before the he was assassinated in Memphis on April 4, 1968.

Powers now says she's the woman. Dr. King's ardent defenders, as they've done before when such allegations have arisen, dispute Powers' claims.

But the oft-asked question is why, after so many years, did Georgia Powers, revered by many Kentuckians and now a senior citizen, go public about an alleged yearlong affair with Dr. King?

"Money, money, money, money," say the snide and cynical.

For her part, Sen. Powers says she wanted relief from the terror under which she's lived for years that she'd be exposed as Dr. King's lover.

"When Dr. King's life is researched, I want the part relating to me to be available in my own words. It is my own history as well, both the good and the bad."

I've read I Shared the Dream from cover to cover. Clearly there's much more to Georgia Davis Powers than her alleged intimacies with one of the world's best-known men.

What's more, I'm inclined to believe that many women over a certain age may even appreciate Sen. Powers' retrospective view of why she became Dr. King's lover:

"I was middle-aged and not feeling very attractive when Martin Luther King, the leader of the civil rights movement, the man who fought so valiantly to make the dream of all Black people for equality a reality, wanted to be with me."

Nonetheless, the way Powers' book is written, packaged and promoted undermines her absolutely correct contention that the contributions of women to the civil rights movement- as strategists, organizers and foot soldiers-have either been downplayed or ignored.

By puffing up alleged intimacies with Dr. King, Powers, intentionally or not, doesn't lift "movement women" up, but diminishes them.

By emphasizing her connection to Dr. King, Powers draws attention away from her own battles against Kentucky's Democratic establishment, which in the early 1960s, had no use for an audacious black woman who dared believe she could be elected senator.

By focusing on intimate nights with Dr. King and on waiting for his calls or for him to send an emissary to fetch her to go wherever he was whenever he wanted her, Powers takes attention away from her tireless efforts to eradicate age, race, class and gender discrimination.

People may long remember that she was Dr. King's lover but may forget Powers' courage in pushing for anti-mask legislation in Kentucky in the face of threats from the Ku Klux Klan.

Sadly, Powers, by her own hand, has written a life story that in many ways contradicts her early yearnings to be a "somebody" in her own right and not simply a woman content to stand in the shadows of a great man.

After reading I Shared the Dream, I recalled my mother's cool response to the wag who came to her with tales about my late father's alleged infidelities. "If you did not come to me with these things when my husband was alive and able to defend himself," she said, "why would you come to me now when he can't?"

Later, my mother told my sisters and me: "Always remember this, he was your father, but he was my man. There are things about our relationship that are none of your business."

Of course, Georgia Davis Powers had every right to write her autobiography as she saw fit, and she did.

However, even for people in public life, there are things that are none of our business-things best left unsaid, left to rumormongers or speculators.

– February 2, 1995

Survivors of the darkest night

ELIE WIESEL speaks so softly that you have to lean in close to make out what he's saying. I did and was rewarded with a feeling I hadn't felt since July 1998, when Rep. John Lewis, a veteran of the civil rights movement, sat in the same spot talking about why and how he's able to love his enemies and to even pray for them.

Wiesel was in town to talk about his book, And the Sea is Never Full: Memoirs 1969 -, at the Kentucky Author Forum sponsored by the University of Louisville. He's written 40 books, but before addressing his larger audience, the 1986 Nobel Peace Prize winner had lunch with members of The Courier-Journal's editorial board.

Wiesel and Lewis are kindred souls. They behave honorably, righteously, morally and lovingly. Yet both endured vicious hatred directed toward them, in Wiesel's case because he's a Jew, and in Lewis' case because he's black.

Unlike some 6 million others, including his parents and a younger sister, Wiesel, who was imprisoned in Auschwitz and Buchenwald, survived the Nazi death camps. He was 16 when finally liberated and didn't know until after the war that his other two sisters had also survived.

Lewis was a youngster growing up in America's segregated South when Wiesel was in the concentration camps in Europe.

page 106

Both Wiesel and Lewis refused to die, refused to succumb to the oft-stated libel that they were members of some subspecies.

Wiesel and Lewis lived to tell their stories and their peoples' stories and to dream of a world better than that of their youths. Each has made a life's work of speaking larger truths to new generations.

Wiesel draws people to his light. It's warm there, and quite frankly, I didn't wish to leave. I wanted to lean in closer and closer and listen to him talk and talk and talk and teach and teach and teach.

In Wiesel's company, as with Lewis, one feels oneself in the presence of goodness.

In a private moment, I asked Wiesel, now an American citizen, how he handles his critics who accuse him of being "too 'Judeocentric.'"

He shrugged, as if to say, "It is their problem, not mine."

Later, I read an interview in which Wiesel said that he's not indifferent to any tragedy or the death of any child. But that in no way contradicts the reality that he's also "profoundly Jewish" and is "profoundly linked to the Jewish people."

I loved Wiesel's non-apology for loving his Jewishness.

Of greater concern, Wiesel said last December in an Israeli newspaper, The Jerusalem Post, are the academics who question the testimony of Holocaust survivors. "The Holocaust is being assaulted," he said, contending that certain scholars and teachers feel as if they must "say something new."

Over lunch, Wiesel discussed the Pope's recent outreach to Jews and admission that the Catholic Church had treated Jews badly over the centuries.

Some Jews were disappointed that the Pope was not more specific in condemning the Catholic Church's role during the Holocaust. But Wiesel said that the truth is that "nobody can accept an apology, only the dead can do it."

As far as he's concerned, "the Pope's gesture was good if it means that the church recognizes that something was wrong in those times." The gesture "doesn't erase everything," he added, but the Pope "deserves our respect and our affection.

Still it pains Wiesel that during his Holocaust nightmare, there were apparently many who knew or suspected but didn't act to stop the carnage.

Why weren't the rail lines over which Jews were transported to death camps bombed and bombed and bombed?

Wiesel insists that President Franklin D. Roosevelt knew, "but it was not on his agenda. The priority was to win the war. It hurts," Wiesel said.

It hurts as well to bear witness close up to the hurt in the piercing eyes that sit below Wiesel's bushy brows. At the end of lunch, I embraced Wiesel and was surprised that this man, who was tough enough to survive horrors that most of us could not imagine, felt soft to the touch.

A critic, Christopher Lehmann-Haupt, in a *New York Times* review, scoffed at Wiesel's humility. It's "professed," he wrote, implying that it is, therefore, contrived and dishonest.

When reading certain passages of Wiesel's latest book, Lehmann-Haupt wrote, "You come away persuaded that Wiesel is not entirely innocent of political skills and that his motives for entering the public arena are not all connected to self-sacrifice."

Frankly, it doesn't bother me that Wiesel gets paid for his labors. I get paid, and so does Lehmann-Haupt. All of us who are writers, in one way or another, peddle our memories. It comes through in the topics we select, the words we choose and the people we say are our heroes.

Wiesel is living proof that one person can simultaneously remember and move forward.

All of us, I suspect, who were around the luncheon table with Elie Wiesel experienced his humility, his humanity, as real and refreshing. I am reminded that some people doubted Martin Luther King Jr.'s humility. And he died broke.

– April 13, 2000

Brother in the Court?

It's truly bizarre:

The idea that a black woman, Professor Anita Hill, stands accused of "lynching" a black man, Judge Clarence Thomas, whose staunchest allies include such "good friends" of African Americans as Republican Sens. Strom Thurmond of South Carolina and Orrin. Hatch of Utah.

Oh, how clever are George Herbert Walker Bush and his political machine!

They sliced and diced Anita Hill so thoroughly that if these had been biblical times, I suspect the University of Oklahoma law professor would have been stoned, with black people hurling the largest rocks.

Still I'm shocked and chagrined by the level of hostility many African Americans express for Hill because she dared allege that Thomas, the darling of political conservatives, sexually harassed her 10 years ago.

Ironically, some of the most negative comments about Anita Hill-such things as, "She just wanted Clarence Thomas for herself and decided to get even after he married that white woman"-have come from the mouths of black women.

And also ironically, some of these same women say they've also been sexually harassed, but wouldn't dare publicize it if it meant pulling a "black brother" down.

Suddenly, Clarence Thomas is a "black brother."

Is this the same Clarence Thomas who lied about the extent of his sister and her children's welfare dependency?

Is this the same Clarence Thomas whose family was lying low in Pin Point, Ga. while he lived high on the hog in Washington, D.C.?

page 109

Is this the same Clarence Thomas who, as head of the Equal Employment Opportunity Commission, allowed dozens of discrimination cases, many of them filed by his black brothers and sisters, to languish and die?

Is this the same Clarence Thomas who sat up in front of white America acting as if his rise from poverty was some singular achievement, accomplished because he, unlike the rest of us black folks, wasn't shiftless and lazy?

I dare say Thomas doesn't often use the term "black brother" unless it's politically expedient to do so. And that's precisely what he did by appealing to the deepest emotions of African Americans, especially black men, by alleging that Anita Hill, a black woman, was part of some dark conspiracy to lynch him for being "uppity."

He may have forgotten much about being black, exploited and discriminated against, but Thomas hasn't forgotten the magic words. He knows how sensitive we are when one of our own claims he's being lynched or is the victim of a racist plot. He knows that many of us cry every time we hear Billie Holiday wail about the "strange fruit" she saw swinging from a Southern tree.

And Thomas is surely aware of and has shamefully exploited the emotional topic of whether there is indeed a real conspiracy to destroy black men and boys.

Just like his buddy in the White House, Thomas knew that many African Americans, who haven't read his speeches or reviewed his disgraceful record at EEOC, would blindly rush to his defense when he twisted up his face, shed crocodile tears, looked truly injured, and uttered the magic words.

I've heard black people say they weren't for Thomas before Hill's allegations, but changed their minds after watching the hearings and seeing "Brother" Clarence's emotional reaction.

Indeed, some people were less concerned about Hill's allegations than they were that she, in their words, "aired our dirty laundry" in public.

What is it about us that white folks don't already know? After all, since the first African stumbled off a slave ship, black people haven't had any privacy. Hasn't anyone but me noticed that there's a cottage industry of "experts" on African Americans?

I've learned many lessons in recent weeks, and one valuable one is never to underestimate George Bush's political machine. He, Thurmond, Hatch and Thomas played African Americans better than Dizzy Gillespie blows a horn; better than Aretha Franklin sings; and better than Toni Morrison writes.

Hopefully, there's a silent majority of black women who feel like my friend Carol Ralph, who says every black woman ought to register to vote and then vote out all those congressmen who got over at our expense.

Meanwhile, I ask: How long will we African Americans sit still and allow black hustler-politicians like Clarence Thomas to prostitute our legitimate hurts and long history of oppression?

We may never know for sure whether "Brother" Clarence sexually harassed Anita Hill. But what we do know is that he knows, she knows, and God knows, and it's been my experience that God has a way of fixing things.

– October 24, 1991

McNamara: Vietnam's last casualty?

IN MY MIND'S eye I can see them.

Marshall: Wafer-thin. Light brown-skinned. Loved to laugh. Eddie: Puerto Rican. Dark-haired. Handsome. A real charmer. Guy: Tall. Thin. The color of a Hershey bar. A budding journalist.

But I'll never know if Marshall, Eddie and Guy would have matured into fine men, into husbands any woman would be proud to have, or into fathers who would have been the role models many clamor for. Marshall, Eddie and Guy are dead. They're among the more than 58,000 Americans killed in Vietnam.

And there's George, who got hooked on drugs in Vietnam and remained an addict for 30 years. There's Harold and Glen. They didn't physically die in the war, but they left their minds in Vietnam.

For my generation, Vietnam is the sore that festers.

Whether it arises as an issue in a political campaign – who served and who ducked – or in the just-published memoirs of a major player in the war like former Defense Secretary Robert S. McNamara, Vietnam can still elicit frowns and shouts across an editorial conference table.

McNamara's memoir, *In Retrospect: The Tragedy and Lessons of Vietnam,* is a resurrection of rage. It's a book of special significance since McNamara was uniquely positioned to do something about it.

Page 112

As *New York Times* writer R.W. Apple Jr. reminded us, McNamara, defense secretary from 1961 through 1968, "pushed so hard for deeper American military involvement in 1964 and 1965 that the conflict in Southeast Asia became known as "'McNamara's War.'"

Now, three decades later, the hawk no longer flies. At 78, he's declawed, preparing to meet his Maker, and no doubt is concerned about his place in history. The hawk has broken his silence and has landed with a thud.

The one-time nemesis of the doves, the man who called war protesters un-American, now says escalating the fighting in Vietnam was wrong.

But it was more than wrong; it was evil. Evil despite McNamara's assessment that his errors and those of others in power weren't errors "of values and intentions, but of judgment and capabilities."

But it is evil, shaky values, and even a lack of human decency, that allowed McNamara to remain publicly mute when the intelligence available to top brass as early as 1963 was that Vietnam was not a winnable war. They knew then that Vietnam wasn't really a major threat to the U.S. position in Southeast Asia.

McNamara regrets that facts were ignored, that debates that should have been held weren't. He stayed publicly tight-lipped even as President Johnson, McNamara wrote, "made choices that locked the United States onto a path of massive military intervention" that destroyed Johnson's presidency "and polarized America like nothing since the Civil War."

Whose sons were on the battlefields? To be sure, many were the sons of the so-called ghettos, sons of the hollers of Kentucky and West Virginia. What these young men shared was economic class and a lack of juice to evade the draft.

Now freed from the motivation that propels John Wayne-types who never admit mistake or defeat, the old hawk apologizes to the likes of Marshall, Eddie and Guy, who can't hear him. He sheds crocodile tears and says very sorry to the thousands of young men who donated arms, legs, minds, marriages and idealism to the war in Vietnam.

Is McNamara entitled some compassion? There is, after all, great truth in saying that hindsight is 20-20. Is the old hawk entitled to some appreciation that he was a man of his time, when the prevailing view was that might, in particular United States might, was invariably right, and that the big, with impunity, could bully the small and win?

Is McNamara entitled to a nation's gratitude because unlike others, he didn't go to his grave keeping his secrets, but has put Vietnam into context, not merely for future generations, but for the generation that fought and also protested that nasty war?

McNamara is entitled to compassion and yes, even thanks at this late date, for finally finding courage to say: "We were wrong, terribly wrong."

Compassion because he has been and likely will be for the rest of his days the ultimate prisoner of war.

Meanwhile, I'll cherish what the songwriter referred to as my "misty, watercolored memories" of the way Marshall, Eddie, Guy, Harold, Glen and George were, the way we all were before Vietnam interrupted our lives with its demand that young men pay debts they do not owe.

– April 13, 1995

Chapter Eight:

Weeping may endure ...

A mother's love, a mother's sentence

SO, YOU were saying that you really love your mother?"

"Yes ma'am, I do. I really love her. My mother raised me by herself, and she made a lot of sacrifices for me."

"Well, little man, that's a great speech. But I don't believe that you love your mother."

"You can't say that!"

"I'm saying it, and I can back it up."

"How? You don't know my life story."

"You're right. I don't know the details of your life. But wasn't that your mother a few nights ago on television pleading for your life?

"Wasn't that photo on the front page of the newspaper a shot of your mother crying as she explained to strangers how she tried to raise you right?

"Wasn't it your mother who said that she had prayed for you? Had asked her Heavenly Father for mercy and asked the jury in your murder case to have mercy as well?"

"Yes, but..."

"But nothing. A proud woman was reduced to an emotional heap when she sat before a judge, jury, cameras and reporters, struggling to make strangers believe that you couldn't be a murderer, or an accessory to murder, because you are her son, and she raised you right."

"Yes, but you don't understand. You see..."

"No, little man, it's you who doesn't understand. The news reports say that you showed no emotion in court. Maybe that's because you still don't grasp the enormity of your situation. Don't yet grasp the mother love that your mother has for you and that the mother of the boy you're accused of having had a hand in killing had for her son.

"And now he's dead. And for what? A pair of sneakers? A cheap thrill?

"No, little man, you don't understand mother love just yet, but eventually you will.

"In the meantime, your mother's sentence is living with knowledge that you're locked up with who knows whom. And I suppose that she'll come to visit. She may be tired, but she'll come. She may be angry, but she'll come.

She may be embarrassed and humiliated, but she'll come. I imagine that she'll visit you even after your friends have forgotten all about you.

"Mothers do those sorts of things. Mothers see good when others see evil. Mothers see potential when others see hopelessness.

"And forever and a day, little man, your mother will pray for you. But she won't be there if ever the hour arrives that some lifer in the next cell over decides that you would make him a fine girlfriend.

"Your mother's sentence is a lifetime of tears. A lifetime of trying to live with the knowledge that the world believes that she gave birth to a murderer."

"But, you don't understand, I didn't...I only..."

"You're right. I don't understand how you can claim to love your mother and yet bring down upon her such suffering and grief, such shame and sorrow.

"And to think, this pain has been inflicted on the one who did not abort you. On the one who lay down and labored until finally a doctor said, 'Mother, you can rest now. It's a boy!'

"All this heartache for the one who endured the scorn of the gossips who talk badly about young girls who get pregnant and aren't married. This is the mother who now is sentenced to act as if she doesn't hear those wagging tongues whispering as she passes, 'See, I told you so.'

"Your mother loves you, little man. Some, in fact, may

argue that perhaps if your mother loved you less, corrected you more often, didn't always make excuses for you, that you might not be where you are now, and she might never have had to look another grieving mother in the face who says that you are responsible for her pain and grief."

These were some of my thoughts as I read and watched television coverage of the trial in Louisville that resulted from the slaying last August of a beautiful 15-year-old named Quintin Hammond.

Quintin's death wasn't a case of gang warfare, or a drug deal gone awry.

Rather, the prosecutor surmised that Quintin, a popular football player who was on his way to school, was "stalked" as if he were an animal who happened into the gun sights of a hunter on safari.

"It was a senseless, brutal murder of a totally, wholly, completely innocent human being," the prosecutor said.

Unfortunately, we've heard this story before.

In recent years, all across this nation, hundreds of mothers, with varying degrees of parenting skills, have cried oceans of tears for slain sons and for sons found guilty of murder. And in practically every case, we're reminded of a mother's capacity to love, and love fiercely, even the child whom others have deemed a remorseless predator.

Editor's Note: Quintin Hammond's young murderer served time in a juvenile facility until he turned 18. He has been transferred to an adult prison and will be eligible for parole in 12 years.

– June 4, 1998

Protecting a daughter's love

HER FATHER, William Jefferson Clinton, is the most powerful man in the world: He's President of the United States. My father, George Washington Winston, held no formal titles, except Daddy. Still, I can identify with Chelsea Clinton because I adored my father too.

And so I was deeply hurt when, around the age of 15, one of my supposed girlfriends informed me that she had overheard her mother telling someone else's mother that my father had a girlfriend. She was smirking when she said it, and I wanted to smack her face, but my spirit was too crushed.

Instead, I ran home crying. By the time I reached our apartment, I was hysterical. "What in the world?" my mother asked, figuring that I had been in a playground fight. I wanted my mother to make the pain go away. I wanted

her to say, "A girlfriend? Not your father!" But to this day, I don't really know whether my father had a girlfriend or not. My mother, you see, never said yes and she never said no. Instead, she explained that some people love to carry tales-love to say things they know will hurt you. What's more, she said, it was possible that some of my friends were jealous because my father was at home, and theirs weren't.

My mother dried up my tears by reminding me that my father loved us and worked hard to take care of us and to keep us off welfare. My father was a good man who sometimes drank too much. And when men drink too much, my mother said, they're not always conscious of what they're doing, and sometimes they may fall asleep in other people's houses.

Bless her heart, my mother talked me through the crisis. Perhaps she cried after I went downstairs. But I felt stronger because of her reassurances.

I realize now that my father was nobody's angel, and that my mother obviously took that into account when she married him in 1945 and while she remained with him until his death. For women of my mother's generation, a hard-working, steady-working man was worth his weight in gold. And my father's gold standard was all the higher because, although he was a drinker, he was never physically abusive to my mother or his children.

My mother never made a federal case out of my father's weaknesses, not even after he died. As a matter of fact, as my father's life neared its end, he attempted to apologize, but my mother told him that apologies to her weren't necessary because his sins were not hers to judge; they were ultimately between my father and his God.

Listening to all the pontificating about how Hillary and Chelsea Clinton are weathering the storm of President Clinton's sexual escapades, I've thought about my parents' relationship. I'm sure that it isn't easy for mother or daughter. But as embarrassed as she no doubt must be, I'm inclined to believe that Chelsea Clinton probably loves her father as much as she ever did. And that maybe her mother, like mine, has said a time or two, "Don't worry, Chelsea. This isn't your battle to fight. Your father loves you."

I'm also inclined to believe that Hillary Clinton, as many mothers do in such times, has created a safe emotional space for Chelsea that cannot be easily penetrated by those who don't care or understand.

Fortunately for most parents, the President among them, how much your children love you doesn't depend on your perfection. I loved and respected my father because that's what I was raised to do. My love for him never was lessened by the world's assessment of him as a poor black alcoholic. I loved my father because I never doubted that my father loved me. His weaknesses, as I came to understand them, were separate from his relationship with me.

And I appreciate all the more my mother protecting the love and respect she wanted my sisters and me to have for her husband and our father. To have stopped loving my father because he had faults, or because of the ugly things neighbors said to make me cry, would have been to disrespect my mother's decision to keep us together as a family.

Perhaps Chelsea Clinton feels similarly.

My mother could have walked away, but she didn't. And by staying, she taught me about compassion and forgiveness. And who better to learn about such things than from the one who brought me into the world? And who better to learn it from than from the one who, at the times when I didn't measure up, had compassion and forgiveness for me? My mother was just one of those women who really meant it when she married my father for richer or poorer, for better or worse, and in sickness and health.

Perhaps Hillary Clinton is too.

– October 1, 1998

The passing of a mighty woman

WE'VE ALL heard plenty "I knew Betty Shabazz" stories. This all reminds me of how after Betty Shabazz's husband, Malcolm X, was assassinated in 1965, all manner of strangers claimed, "I was with Malcolm." But they weren't.

Betty Shabazz was my sister in the Delta Sigma Theta Sorority Inc. We were once members of the same chapter, New York Alumnae. Betty Shabazz was also a friend of my mentor, and their relationship provided other opportunities for me to be in Betty's company.

However, I dare not profess that Betty Shabazz and I were best of friends.

Rather, like others, I admired her, was awed by her, and stayed back a respectful distance from which I watched and learned.

Of course, since the fatal fire at her home, reportedly set deliberately by Shabazz's 12-year-old grandson, Malcolm, my sorority sister has accumulated many, many new good friends.

Based on the occasions that we crossed paths, I could say amen to Attallah Shabazz's comment soon after her mother died.. "Dr. Betty Shabazz," Attallah said, "has made a transition, but is very mighty where she is. She's strong where she is."

That's always how Betty Shabazz seemed to me.

Of course, whatever anyone thinks or says now about Betty Shabazz is inconsequential to her. She's free now from all our weak judgments-and from the phonies who'll now say that they loved her.

Page 121

Right now, it is Betty Shabazz's daughters who need support and prayers. In many black families, it still is nothing but the might of a mother that keeps them going. It's that might that keeps daughters believing that no matter what the doctors say, Mother will not die.

I can appreciate Betty Shabazz's daughters' instruction that doctors be aggressive in trying to save her life. Anyone who has been there appreciates how it takes time to imagine a world without Mother to fight your battles.

By struggling to live, Betty Shabazz reasserted her might, and survived longer than anyone had any right to expect from one who had suffered third-degree burns over 80 percent of her body. Each day that she survived was not, for those who kept a vigil, a day that put Betty closer to death; it was a day that put her closer to life.

Which of the six, I wonder, will emerge from behind the giant shadow Betty Shabazz cast to become mother to the group? It's not necessarily age. It's not always the case that the oldest is the wisest or that the youngest knows the least.

Malcolm X and Betty Shabazz's daughters now will be challenged to keep loving one another, especially the one among them who seems to needs mothering the most. Indeed, Betty's death, and the circumstances, may only exaggerate her need.

Five of those six women will be challenged to keep loving the one who taxed Mother the most-the one whose overwhelming needs at times may have meant that there wasn't always enough of Mother to go around.

There are many theories about how Qubilah Shabazz, and her son, little Malcolm, who now may be charged with murder, ended up so troubled. If it's true that Qubilah never recovered from seeing her father murdered 32 years ago, then she's really not so different than others whose experienced childhood traumas.

But despite Qubilah's troubles, Betty Shabazz never willingly invited curiosity-seekers into her children's private lives. That is only fitting for one who was mighty.

I've heard that Betty Shabazz was never told that her grandson set the fire.

If so, I'm glad, because God really does know just how much one mighty woman can bear.

Rest in peace, Sister Betty.

– June 26, 1997

The zigzag road of Tupac's mom

WHILE IN LOUISVILLE, Afeni Shakur, former Black Panther, recovering addict and mother of slain superstar rapper Tupac Shakur, proved not to be an easy interview. Shakur, all 118 pounds of her, stood fierce against the standard lines of inquiry that too often demand people who live complex lives to explain themselves simplistically.

So when asked if she ever urged her son to keep profanity out of his music, Shakur articulated opposition to censorship. "That was his art," she said.

"I never felt like I wanted to stymie his development."

Asked if she's spoken with the family of slain rapper "Biggie" Smalls-a reported rival of Tupac who was gunned down in similar fashion to Tupac six months later-Shakur could barely hide her impatience with the question.

Instead, Shakur reminded the 1,500 or so young people attending St. Stephen Baptist Church's second annual youth conference that mothers of slain rappers aren't the only mothers grieving. Violence is not a creation of young people or rap music, she said.

"Sept. 13, 1996," Shakur said, "was the day that death visited my home. I feel that we come here with a beginning date and an ending day. . . . I lost my only son. Obviously, that's devastating."

Rejecting the comfortable chair set on the stage for her, Shakur instead stood among the young people. She actually seemed to draw fire and raw energy from them. Indeed, the presence of so many, she said was a miracle because, "This is not a school class; you made a choice to be here."

Shakur talked openly about her years living in a haze of drugs. "I was just trying to dull my pain," she said.

Shakur recalled December 1990 when she weighed just 86 pounds and arrived back in New York City by bus from California, where she had been getting high. "I was sitting on the floor of [the] Port Authority [terminal], surrounded by five big bags, and I'll never forget my family coming to retrieve me-coming to retrieve their trash."

By 1993, Shakur's life was finally coming together. She said that Tupac, by then famous, asked her to become his publicist. The passing of four years hasn't seemed to dull Shakur's amazement at her son's request.

"My son asked me to help him, and I could help!" she said.

Nowadays, Shakur said she's born again.

"I rejoice in the prospect of living another day. But that was only after I was broken down. For the last six years, I have been clean and sober. The last five or six years of my son's life, he got to spend with his real mama."

Afeni Shakur talked bluntly about, as she termed it, "the garbage in my life." But she wasn't readily responsive to a question that implied that perhaps the poor choices she made in her life could be responsible for her son's violent end.

"Tupac Amaru wasn't a crack addict, I was," Shakur said firmly. "Tupac became who he was in spite of his mother."

And don't ask her to speak for Tupac. "If you want to know what Tupac thought about anything, you need to go and listen to him," she said. "I do not find it necessary to explain my son; my son was real good at explaining himself."

When she was asked what she says to young people inclined to following Tupac's footsteps, Shakur did not speak about role models. Rather, she trained her eyes on the young audience and said, "Tupac wanted to change the economic face of this community. He didn't have to do that.

You don't have to follow in anybody's footsteps. You can become leaders."

And it was with equal firmness that Shakur said to the youths about the violence that took her son's life and the lives of so many others, "You are not old enough to have invented teen violence."

That Afeni Shakur did not always follow the script demanded by some of the questions that were put to her apparently confused some onlookers, and they talked about it later.

But peering down at her from the balcony of St. Stephen, one could see a woman still in transition, still fresh to sobriety.

One can look upon Afeni Shakur and see embodied in one tiny, dark frame many of the complexities, and yes, the stark contradictions of one who has trod a zigzag path and is yet in the process of finding her way back from the messes she's made.

Look and listen to Afeni Shakur and be reminded of the many addicted, unwed women among us who are trying to raise children, and who sometimes miraculously get it right, but often get it wrong. It's an easy temptation to assign them all the blame, without demanding to know what caused their pain.

If Afeni Shakur is a role model for anything, it might be that her life helps shatter the myth, which apparently took root during slavery, that black women are impervious to pain and are resilient under every circumstance.

It's not always been a badge of honor that black women were the original supermoms. Indeed, black women like Afeni Shakur aren't always sympathetic figures to people who have never had to walk in their shoes.

– May 28, 1997

A woman in combat

WHY DOESN'T Winnie Mandela confess, apologize and move on?

This is a fair question. And it's a question being asked by millions who have followed Winnie Mandela's life, who have been awed and inspired by her valor. Those questioners now find themselves pained that one of history's great warriors may end up being remembered less for her courage under fire than for the possibility that she's been driven a bit mad by the insane, racist and evil political system that she dedicated her life to overthrowing.

The allegations against Winnie Mandela are serious. And I suspect that what upsets many people who watched Winnie Mandela's performance before South Africa's Truth and Reconciliation Commission is that she betrays no hint of contrition. Though accused of all sorts of crimes, including kidnapping, torture and even murder, Winnie Mandela probably appears to some observers as a general who had a war to fight and win, but who had little time or patience for the sentimentalities and clear logic of peacetime.

What's more, I'm sure that for some it is also unnerving to see these supposedly masculine traits in a woman.

The testimony against Winnie Mandela, the former wife of South African President Nelson Mandela, was riveting and revolting. But it was not without the contradictions that a deft defense attorney might be able to fashion into a winnable court case.

One man testified that he saw Mrs. Mandela plunge a tiny object into 14-year-old Stompe Moekhetsi Seipei. But the man who confessed to the killing and who described it in gruesome detail did not finger Mrs. Mandela as the killer, but as the inspiration for the crime.

If Winnie Mandela is guilty of all that she's been accused, one might wonder whether her path to confession and apology is blocked by the hell apartheid made of her life, her husband's life, her marriage, her children's lives, and the lives of all black South Africans.

When people play Monday-morning quarterback relative to Winnie Mandela, they may wish to remember that under apartheid, nothing was normal in South Africa. Winnie Mandela and others in the African National Congress,

including Nelson Mandela, saw themselves first and foremost as soldiers in a war, as freedom fighters. When they were arrested, the world outside South Africa perceived them, plain and simple, as political prisoners.

Nelson Mandela spent 27 years in prison for his anti-apartheid activities, but Winnie Mandela's life outside the walls involved more suffering than simply a woman separated from her man, a mother separated from her husband.

She was a woman in combat.

And we know, or should, that war and the suffering in war have a way of distorting reality, and that if the war goes on long enough, it is possible for the soldiers no longer to be able to realize the difference between right and wrong, good and evil. This is not to excuse Winnie Mandela. It's simply to say that a fair assessment of her must take her suffering over such a long period distorted her proper perceptions.

Winnie Mandela is in her sixties, but those who have studied her life come away assured that this woman has actually lived a thousand years, and maybe has died a couple thousand times.

Imagine years of being spied on, detained, banned, harassed, cursed, spat upon, hauled into court and repeatedly jailed, including the first time in 1958, when she was pregnant. Imagine being declared by the government a non-person, placed under house arrest, and banned from chatting with a neighbor over the fence, having a friend over for tea or talking on the telephone without the government's permission.

Imagine as well what it must have been like for Winnie Mandela to see her children routinely frightened, ridiculed and harassed by grown men while her husband was languishing in prison.

Is it possible that the years of being at war-the years of struggling to keep mind, family and nation together-finally proved too much and that even the steel-willed Winnie Mandela psychologically collapsed? What's the possibility that her pain is too deep and her memories too fresh to be easily overcome, even though the war has ended and her side has won?

Maybe she remembers that day long ago when, with her daughters, then 4 and 5, she struggled to catch a last glimpse of Nelson before he was hustled off to prison to serve a life sentence. She described her ordeal in her book, Part of My Soul Went With Him.

"I held Zendi's hand and Zindzi was on my arm, when someone grasped my shoulder. I turned and what do I see? A huge policeman, a member of the Security Branch, and he says, 'Remember your permit! You must be back in Johannesburg by 12 o'clock!' Here I was with my people, singing the national anthem, and there was this man with his hand on my shoulder repeating that I must go back to Johannesburg! All I could do was to kick and ignore him. Can you imagine! The last day! My husband is sentenced to life, and I must think of permits and the time of day."

Maybe Winnie Mandela is still haunted by her stints in jail, where she said black prisoners were served food that was uncooked and garnished with bird droppings. As a result, she said, she became malnourished and plagued with bleeding gums and blackouts.

"No human being," she said, "can take those humiliations without reacting."

People who find it difficult to understand why Winnie Mandela, if she is guilty, cannot bring herself to confess may find a clue in a comment made years ago when apartheid raged.

"In the white courts, we never plead guilty to any offense, no matter how petty or how much of a frame-up; this would lower the morale of the people," she said. "And in any case, you cannot plead in mitigation if you are actually innocent and those who accuse you are the real criminals."

– Dec. 11, 1997

Who can find an empowered woman?

Charm can be deceptive and beauty doesn't last, but a woman who fears and reverences God shall be greatly praised.
– Proverbs 31:30

IT DOESN'T GET much harder than being a black woman in a white man's world.

Wrong color. Wrong sex. Too often despised. Underappreciated, if appreciated at all. When there's disease, we often have more of it, suffer worse and die sooner.

Black women. Too often defined as the most unbeautiful. The most unworthy to be loved. The images of us are too often as neck-swiveling, eye-rolling, hip-shaking, sassy-talking, baby-making, "ain't got no man"-complaining

folks. We're too loud, too black, too fat, so get back. Hair too short, too nappy. Nose too wide, feet too big-just too imperfect to be perfect.

Colored girls contemplate suicide but don't have time to die. So bombarded nonetheless by negative messages, we sometimes forget that we serve a Master who knows where the light goes when we flip off the switch and who sees even better in the dark.

So bombarded by negative messages are black girls and black women that we forget that women who look just like us, hurt just like us, and were despised just like us still managed to make a way out of no way. They pressed on to the rhythm of whispers saying, "Ain't no bad experience, baby, just good lessons," or "Baby girl, you don't have to give them your gifts."

Page 131

And as our brother T.D. Jakes has written, "There are some things that a lady can only receive from within herself," and "when human hands fail, there is always strength in the everlasting arms of God."

That's Good News for despised, misunderstood women. To know that we're not really alone as long as there is God. That we're never really powerless as a long as God sits high on the throne and looks low into places where we sometimes try to hide.

What must we do to reorder our steps so we won't keep traveling down the same dead-end streets, always wondering why we always seem to get what we always got?

For one, as Brother Jakes said, "Sometimes we are in pursuit without prayer." We're doing the wrong things for the wrong reasons with the wrong people at the wrong time. We are chained to yesterday. Haunted by and dragging along every hurt we've ever had. Can't go forward for looking back, forgetting, as Brother Jakes also has said, that our God "believes in the least likely" and "invests in the faulty."

But the unempowered woman isn't having a love affair with herself. Instead, she's always looking for love in the wrong places. She believes the hype that she's un-pretty, undesirable, unable. She wears old hurts like a corset that others can see in her walk, hear in her talk, and see in her eyes that look down more than up and in her smiles that too often dissolve into frowns.

An unempowered woman tries to hide it, but her jealousy breaks through.

Never can seem to fix her mouth to say a kind word about the preacher or his wife. Always finding some nit to pick, and inevitably saying at the day's end, "If I were in charge, I would have . . ."

An unempowered woman always has excuses. She's silent when she should be speaking up and running her mouth when she should be still. She's scared a lot of the time and rarely steps out on faith.

An unempowered woman can easily be manipulated and used against herself and her sisters. She has talent, but is terrified to let her light shine-people might come to expect more from her. She is so afraid of her potential that she settles, often not even for second best, but third, fourth or fifth best.

Simply put, an unempowered woman is a mess to behold and to be around. She can't hardly pray for crying. Can't hardly testify for sighing. Afraid to shout for the whole world to hear, "Father, I stretch my hands to thee. I can't do it by myself."

But who among us hasn't ever felt unempowered? Who hasn't sometimes been blindsided by the devil? Felt uninspired and caged like some beast at the zoo?

But after all the crying and sighing is done, an empowered woman puts herself back into the race. She remembers that God loves her and that her mother and the old church ladies always used to say, "If you take one step, God will take two."

Empowered woman make things happen, get things done, and are marvels to behold. Empowered women learn from their mistakes, and leave the garbage in the trashcan. They know that not everyone who starts out with them will finish the race.

An empowered woman acts to turn pain into joy and failure into triumph. She leaves vengeance to the Lord. She demands quiet time. She splurges on occasion for a facial, a massage or a pedicure.

Empowered women deal with the hand that life dealt them, and they have names like Mary, Martha, Naomi, and Ruth. There's Leah, Hagar and Sarah, and Mama, Mommy, Mom, and Ma'Dere. They're called Grandma, Godmother, and Auntie. She's Regina, Kim, Shenequah and Baby Sis.

But ultimately, it doesn't matter what we call ourselves, as long as it's good and as long as we know who God is and who and whose we are. As long as we know and proclaim that God is the Alpha and the Omega, the Rose of Sharon, the Lily of the Valley, the Lord of Lords, the King of Kings, and the Omnipotent One.

Simply put, an empowered woman decides not to be powerless, and when such feelings do creep in, she knows what she has to do: She falls down on her knees, and she prays.

– 1998

A tribute to a blackbird who has flown away

Mother. Grandmother. Daughter. Sister. Sister-in-law. Friend. Confidante. My dear Sister/Girlfriend.

No, you didn't.

Granted, you have a sense of drama.

But really. Now you did not just up and fly away. Just leave us back here with our mouths hung open and our hearts hung heavy.

No long or even short goodbyes. Sister/Girlfriend, you just up, in an instant, and took leave.

We looked away for a moment and you were gone. Just rushed off to glory on the wings of a horse called Faith to a place where we've been promised there is no more pain.

We should be angry at you for leaving us like this. Didn't you know that we love you?

Didn't you know that without you we won't know how to make sense out of what Toni Morrison really means when she gets down and deep? And how are we, without you, ever going to be able to figure out what Alice Walker is truly trying to say?

Sister girl, we'll never read or hear read another Nikki Giovanni poem and not think of you and smile. Yeah, as Nikki has written, you were our "Cotton Candy on a Rainy Day."

page 135

We'll never recite Maya Angelou's "Still I Rise," and not envision you smiling and saying, "Go on girl with your bad self!"

But you knew, didn't you, Sister girl how loved you were, how loved you are.

Guess that's why there wasn't any need for you to tarry or even stop and pack. You just up and left, and flew away like a blackbird, with whatever you had on your back.

How many times do we have to be told at time like this that as much as we love one another, there's someone who loves us better. There's someone who gives life and takes life, replacing it with eternal life and peaceful rest.

Even if our faith can be squeezed into an itty-bitty mustard seed it's enough to know that the last time we saw you wasn't the last time for those who have the faith. For those who seek to experience God's pure love.

You have seen God's face, and if we're fortunate, one day we all make the same journey. You just sashayed on up there in flowing African robes.

Oh, Sister girl, if we can not be blinded by our tears, we can look just over yonder and imagine you in God's heaven, with God smiling when you toss your head back and rap about 'dem hips, 'dem marvelous hips that He gave you in the first place.

I can imagine you up there in the by and by sipping tea with Zora Neale Hurston and filling her in on what's been happening down here since she's been gone. I can hear you reassuring Baldwin saying, "James, some people have just arrived where you were 30 years ago."

Oh, I can see you poeting with Audre Lourde and Toni Cade Bambara.

Yeah, right about now, there's a slammin' African-American Read-in heaven, and the audience includes Langston Hughes, Richard Wright, Ralph Ellison, John Oliver Killens and Larry Neal, still bebopping.

You got your invitation, and our invites are in the mail, to be delivered whenever God gets ready. And up there in heaven's library are all the books that you would ever hope to have gathered in one place, and God has given you eternity to read.

My dear Sister/Girlfriend, you gave so much of yourself to so many in your short stay on earth, so it's no wonder that your heart just gave out. But for whatever reason God called your name before ours, we who believe know that God doesn't make mistakes; that he must have wanted you for something and right now.

We're enriched because you lived. We're blessed to have been within your circle of friends, family, colleagues and acquaintances. Sleep on, my dear friend, for surely you've earned your place in our hearts and your eternal rest.

– Adaptation of a eulogy written for sister-writer M. Celeste Nichols, who was laid to rest on April 12, 1996.

A prayer for self-esteem

If anyone ever asks, "Who do you think you are?" you better have an answer.

If not, the questioner will define you.

Amen.

Acknowledgements

I LEARN A LOT about writers when I read who and what they give thanks to and for. So it's become a habit to read acknowledgements. And now that I've written this one, I have greater appreciation for taking time out to say thanks. And as countless writers before me have done, I pray that any who've contributed to this effort but whose names aren't specifically mentioned will know that no slight was intended and that thanks is given for your contributions too.

My thanks go to Wayne Dawkins, founder of August Press, for always believing in me. Kimberly Thompson Henderson, for whom editing *Blackbird* wasn't a job, but a Sister committed to making another Sister look good.

Rob King. You're incredibly talented and soooo busy, so thanks for squeezing time to design the cover, and Keith Williams, an artist with a camera, for the cover photograph.

The Courier-Journal has given me a platform for all these years, and I'm grateful to Ed Manassah, publisher, and David Hawpe, editorial director, for permission to reprint the columns. My colleagues on *The Courier-Journal* editorial board, Jill Johnson Keeney, Bert Emke, Ed Bennett, Laurel Shackelford, Warren Buckler, and, of course, Stephen Ford and Keith Runyon,

who alternate as my editors, and who've saved me from embarrassment many times. Kathy Fowler, thanks for your positive attitude whenever I drop in to chat, and Margery Duvall for ably assisting us all.

Much respect, love and thanks to the late James Aronson of Hunter College, who placed me on the writing path. Also, Hunter professor Arnold Gibbons, who brought the Third World into the classroom and lit a fire that still burns inside of me. Thanks also to Phyl Garland, Luther Jackson and the late Norman Issacs, my teachers and mentors at Columbia University Graduate School of Journalism.

To the Class of 1980: So many of you are doing great things in the worlds of journalism and books. I'm awed

Page 139

and inspired by your talents. You are all the role models I'll ever need. To the members of the Black Alumni Network, we're 20 years old and still going strong.

To *Essence* magazine's second editor Marcia Gillespie for giving a fledging writer a break and Valerie Wilson Wesley, for doing the same later on.

Heartfelt thanks to my first editor in journalism, Nancy Q. Keefe. You cared.

No words are remotely appropriate to express my gratitude in Kathy Skiba, Vanessa Williams and DeWayne Wickham for friendship and sharing and caring down through the years. To my organizations: The National Association of Black Journalists, the William Monroe Trotter collective of African-American opinion writers, Chums of Louisville Inc., the Afrocentric Readers' Circle, Delta Sigma Theta Sorority Inc., and, of course, the Rev. Kevin W. Cosby and the St. Stephen Baptist Church family. Thank you for affirmations.

Mae Jackson: Keep speaking truth to power.

And Sandi Castine's Prayer Circle: We're the evidence that prayer works.

My heart brims with love for the two who encouraged me to go to college and who were there for me all the way: Duane Jones, a gifted actor, who not enough of the world ever got to see perform. You are missed from the planet.

Gerterlyn O. Dozier (initials G.O.D.). Thank you Lyn for every book you ever gave me and for teaching me to drive so that I can leave a party whenever I want to.

Thank you to my village back home, East River projects and the Church of the Ascension. I never forgot where I came from.

Much gratitude to the courageous Brothers and Sisters of the civil rights movement, especially SNCC, for prying open opportunities denied by racism. Special love and appreciation to my first political teacher, Ralph Featherstone. Been mourning and missing his presence for 30 years.

Finally, but surely not least, all praises to the architect of the world and my life. Thank you, God, for answering prayers.

Also by August Press:

Black Journalists: The NABJ Story
Wayne Dawkins, ISBN 0963572040

Welcome to Exit 4: Enter at Own Risk
Rosemary Parrillo, ISBN 0963572016

Goodnight Sweetheart Goodnight:
The Story of the Spaniels
Richard G. Carter, ISBN 0963572024

Sometimes You Get the Bear
Dan Holly, ISBN 0963572059

To order any of these titles
write to P.O. Box 6693
Newport News, VA 23606

Or call (800) 268-4338
Internet: www.augustpress.net